LOCAL SEO SECRETS

20 LOCAL SEO STRATEGIES YOU SHOULD BE USING **NOW**

LOCAL SEO EXPERTS SHARE THEIR TOP STRATEGIES
FOR RANKING FAST AND DRIVING ORGANIC TRAFFIC

ROGER BRYAN

Local SEO Secrets – First Edition 2 1 0
ISBN-13: 978-1-946694-45-4

Library of Congress Control Number: 2020922627

To Claire: Never Stop Trying… Daddy Loves You "Munch"!

Table of Contents

Preface

Why You Should Read This Book

We brought together some of the top minds in the Local SEO space and asked them one simple question: What *is* working (and what *isn't*). This book outlines the Top 20 Strategies they were willing to share.

Visit https://GrowthFoundry.com/Local-Seo-Book before you start reading to sign up to receive an interactive digital copy of this book (free of charge). From here, you can get all of the updates that we publish along with direct access to the professionals who provided the following chapters.

If at any time you get stuck on a topic, you can head over to the Q&A Section of the interactive digital copy or you can text me (no calls, please) on my personal cell phone 202-738-6344 (yes, this is my real number!)

NOTE TO READERS: As this book was being published, my agency Enfusen and its AI-powered SAAS solution were acquired by Growth Foundry. Throughout this book, you'll see references to Enfusen or screenshots associated with that business which have been left as is to avoid publication delays. Some URLs may have been redirected or the pages no longer exist. I apologize in advance if this creates any issues for you.

—Roger Bryan

SECTION 1 – INTRODUCTION

CHAPTER 1

Should You Consider SEO For Your Business?

Before we get started, we probably should define what SEO or search engine optimization is. SEO is an activity that helps you to increase the quality and quantity of visitors to your website. That's the simplest explanation that anyone's going to give you.

As you read this book, you will learn the intricacies and complexities of running an SEO campaign and the efforts required to drive success from doing so.

So, let's first talk about the opportunity. I've outlined seven things that search engine optimization can do for your website and your business that should help you consider whether this is a good fit for you.

1. Helps you build your brand

SEO helps you to tell the world who you are and what you do. You can guide how the world views you based on the keywords in the content you create. There's no better way to create a long-term view of your product, service, or brand than through search engine optimization.

2. Free traffic that tends to stick around

SEO is an investment that pays dividends over time. Often, it drives the lowest cost per acquisition of all traffic sources, meaning it's the least expensive way to drive sales for your business.

3. You don't have to pay for each click

When properly done, SEO tends to improve over time, allowing you to spend less on paid ads. One of the problems with paid ads is when you turn them off, that traffic source completely disappears, and all of those conversions stop. When you properly invest in search engine optimization, you allow yourself to build a traffic source that continues to pay dividends day after day, week after week, month after month, year after year.

4. HELPS BUYERS FIND YOUR SITE BECAUSE IT'S WHERE THEY'RE ALREADY LOOKING

Think about it like this: When your site ranks well, it's like putting your product or service at the front door of Walmart, where everyone will see it as they walk in the store. People are already going to search engines looking for products and services. It's your responsibility as a business owner to make sure that they find you first, and you can accomplish that goal through search engine optimization.

5. INCREASES YOUR CREDIBILITY AND YOUR INDUSTRY AUTHORITY

When you put out good content and share it with site visitors, you become a trusted source of information. People buy from the people that they trust. Again, it's your responsibility as a business owner to be utilizing search engine optimization and sharing your message about your product and service with the world. So, when prospects search for answers to their questions, they find you. You become the trusted source of information, and it makes it easier for them to buy from you in the future.

6. HELPS YOU STAY AHEAD OF AND BEAT YOUR COMPETITION

Each time you outrank a competitor, you increase your chances of taking their business, helping you grow while limiting their growth. This is extremely important. There will be times when you will come against a much larger competitor who has more money than to buy ads. But with a well-executed search engine optimization campaign, you can become at par with or even beat them at their own game and gain the traction and audience that they want to add and deposit those revenues in your pocket.

7. EASY TO MEASURE

SEO is one of the easiest traffic sources to monetize and track. You can track ranks, impressions, visits, and mean conversions easily with a few simple tools, giving you full transparency of your efforts.

The opportunities are immense. The risks are minimal. When done right, search engine optimization is the one traffic source that can pay exponential dividends with long term growth opportunities. It's not something your business can afford to overlook. It's something that you need to take action on today.

In this book, we will show you step-by-step how we implement successful search engine optimization campaigns, the strategies we use, the tools we use, and the data we use to manage that success. Also included are a few hacks to help you get started fast and get those rankings that will help you drive success in your business for years to come.

CHAPTER 2

My Story

My publisher told me I need to tell you a little about myself... If you don't care, I don't blame you. You can skip this chapter, or you can read on. Either way, it won't change how amazing the content is.

I started my SEO career in the late nineties before I realized that's what I was doing. The internet was just beginning to become commercially relevant, so the process of using it to grow and scale a business was in its nascent stages. I would argue that the process of implementing SEO—and its increasing economic value—is similar to any major shift in communication that affects economic output.

You can compare the internet of the late 1990s to the telephone of the late nineteenth century. In 1878, when few people had a phone, a New Haven telephone company printed the first directory with 50 listings, which included every person, business, and organization in the area that had a telephone. Fast forward to 1938—telephones had become a global communication tool, so AT&T commissioned the first new type of phone book that most people are familiar with today. Soon after, companies began using names such as A+ Towing, AAA Cleaning, etc., so they would be listed at the top of the page under each alphabetical category. These companies knew that to get the business, they would need a name that would optimize their listing to come up first. That optimization strategy is very similar to the ways we optimize listings today for search.

Making this historical comparison is key because I believe SEO is deeply misunderstood; it is a data-driven process that iterates a billion times faster than a yearly phone book imprint. If implemented properly, you can scale and grow a business in months, not years.

I know because I've done it.

LEARNING BY DOING – HOW I LAUNCHED MY SEO CAREER

In the late 1990s, the internet was starting to pick up commercial steam. I was on active duty in the Marine Corps, hustling on the side for a communications company that sold long-distance (1-800 numbers) and pagers. I focused on selling them to other Marines and their families. To increase sales, I also recruited these Marines to sell long-distance and pagers as part of a multi-level marketing strategy.

Part of my sales pitch to small businesses included setting up a "page" for them in GeoCities, one of the largest web hosting platforms at that time. I experimented with basic listing strategies for these customers, which I now realize inadvertently launched my SEO career. Quite frankly, no one really understood how web hosting worked or why it was important to have a website.

This was my first attempt at using the internet for sales and an important realization that I later capitalized on while working for other companies and starting my own company.

By the time I was in my late twenties, I'd founded a successful non-profit marketing agency that I owned from 2007-2012. I grew the agency into a $5M a year service business that, over seven years, generated $110M for non-profits such as Goodwill Industries, The Salvation Army, and the American Red Cross. This company made INC Magazine's Fastest Growing Companies in 2010, 2011, and 2012 all from Local SEO.

PIVOTING TO A DATA-DRIVEN APPROACH

When I sold my business in 2012, I noticed major algorithmic changes happening, which prompted me to adjust my business model. I realized I needed to be more data-driven in my Local SEO efforts to get ahead in the industry. It was 2013, and I had recently founded my current company, Enfusen, because I wanted the SEO process to be more reliable. I took the basic SEO approaches that I had previously used to generate millions in revenue and began to uncover the science of creating dependable, predictable revenue streams with data-driven strategies.

For the first three years, we worked with over 700 Microsoft Partners to refine our data-driven approach. In 2016, these strategies generated over $56 million in sales pipeline for these Microsoft Partners.

Also, around that time, we were working with one of the largest healthcare providers in the country (a chain of over 100 hospitals and urgent care facilities) to drive more organic traffic to their sites with high conversion rates in competitive markets such as markets Washington D.C., Baltimore, and New York. On average, we increased organic traffic by 400%, but, more importantly, we increased net new appointments by over 800%. While working with these two major clients, I began to perfect the Data-Driven Local SEO Strategies we use today with our clients.

DATA DRIVES EFFECTIVE SEO

People ask me all the time, "How do you rank a website, and how do you sell SEO services?" It's not an easy answer. There's data and data points. We analyze, understand, and track these data points, and then create a strategy based on that data and nothing else. This book is going to show you exactly how to do that.

The more you understand data in search engine optimization, the greater the opportunity is. Data-driven SEO allows you to understand that every client is different. They're all at a different point in the evolution of their organic traffic generation, and they all need different things. A/B testing the infinite permutations of what might work could take six months to a year. Businesses don't have that kind of time. You have to be able to show some results in 90 days or less.

Understanding SEO data creates real business opportunities. I truly believe anyone can get lucky and rank at least one website for a major keyword and generate traffic. Still, the science behind doing that and creating a dependable, predictable revenue stream from it is very exact, very detailed. It's what inspired me to compile what I've learned into a book to help other marketers who want to be effective.

Working in the field of SEO is both challenging and exciting. You must have a love of learning and the drive to continually improve to stay at the top of your game. The information and insights in this book are meant to set you up for better success, no matter what your marketing role or business goals.

CHAPTER 3

How to Read This Book

This book is a combination of strategies from the Top Local SEO Professionals who are in the trenches working with clients or working to rank their own websites.

If you're not the type of person that likes doing a lot of extra work (I feel you), use this book as a guide for managing the work that others do. As long as you know the right strategy, you can easily hire someone else to do all of the work while managing them intelligently.

As you read each chapter, implement the strategy (or have someone do it for you) and then check off each step to help move you towards increasing your traffic, converting more customers, and growing your business. Each of the implementation chapters includes questions you need to answer before moving to the next chapter. This will help you ensure you do not miss anything that needs to be done to make you successful.

Don't forget to head over to GrowthFoundry.com/local-seo-book to get access to the free interactive digital version of the book where you'll also be able to download your Local SEO Roadmap.

SECTION 2 –
MASTERING THE DATA

CHAPTER 4

THE CORE DATA POINTS
YOU NEED TO SUCCEED

"You can't improve what you don't measure"
– Roger Bryan

Knowing your digital marketing Key Performance Indicators (KPIs) is critical to campaign success.

The foundation of all successful marketing campaigns is an inherent focus on the 'numbers' or KPIs they produce. So, what are the most critical KPIs to consider in a successful Digital Marketing Funnel? We've broken them down into four categories with ten total statistics for you to consider.

Digital Marketing Key Performance Indicators Matrix

THE FOUR CORE ELEMENTS OF DIGITAL MARKETING KPIS

1. RANK

Rank refers to where your keywords rank on Google. The results are assessed primarily using Google Organic and Google Maps rankings to measure the success of your SEO efforts over time.

2. PERFORMANCE

Performance indicators come from the Google Search Console. These data points show how the search engine is presenting your site and how users are reacting to that presentation via different types of interactions.

3. TRAFFIC

Traffic is actual user engagement with your site. Measuring how many people come to the site and how many pages they view during each visit gives you an idea of your opportunity for conversion, shows you which areas need improvement, and which are already doing what they are meant to do.

4. CONVERSION

Conversion is the number of people that take action on your site after visiting. Conversion rates can be measured by phone calls received, form submissions, chat engagements, or other points of financial value capture like sales or return customers.

BREAKDOWN OF TARGET KPIS

1. AVERAGE RANK

When building a digital marketing campaign, you'll work with a select group of keywords that you choose. The success of your efforts in ranking those keywords is monitored at two levels.

The first is 'all keywords,' which shows you the overall success of your efforts. The goal is to have an average rank below 10, meaning all of your keywords are on the first page of Google for either organic position or maps positions.

The second level is the 'keyword group' level, which allows you to measure the success of your efforts around a subset of all keywords, typically relating to a specific URL on your site. By measuring at this detailed level, you can find optimization opportunities in both onsite content and offsite link building, and further narrow the focus of each campaign to help ensure success.

2. VISIBILITY SCORE

Your visibility score is the percentage of keywords that rank on the first page of Google. This is similar to the average rank but takes a slightly different point of view. While average rank will show you the overall scope of success, it can be skewed if a select group of keywords is in the top spot (number 1 for organic or maps) while other keywords are ranking 50+ (or not at all). The visibility score allows you to get a feel for how many keywords you should be working on vs. which specific keywords (as shown with average rank by URL) are the current focus.

The goal is for 80% of keywords to rank on the first page. If you are not reaching that goal, you may want to look at the total number of keywords. Doing less now will help you get better results later.

3. IMPRESSIONS

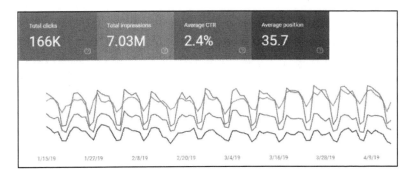

Impressions are the number of times your website is shown within search results. The example shows that this site had 7M impressions over the last 90 days. These results are considered "auditions," where Google has given web searchers the option to click on your site based on the website's relevance to the intent of searchers. The goal is to grow your impression count between 10% every 90 days and 25% on an annualized basis.

4. CLICK-THROUGH RATE (CTR)

The click-through rate is the percentage of people (impressions) who click on your website when given a chance. The key elements that you can control here are your Page Title and Meta Description.

By looking at each page in Google Search Console, you can find opportunities to improve your titles and descriptions to make them more relevant and engaging to the searching audience. The target here is a 3% CTR.

5. PAGEVIEWS

Page	Pageviews	Unique Pageviews
All Users	113,461 % of Total: 100.00% (113,461)	93,403 % of Total: 100.00% (93,403)
Organic Traffic	42,857 % of Total: 37.77% (113,461)	33,503 % of Total: 35.87% (93,403)

Pageviews tell us the number of pages that users visited on your site in a given time frame, which gives us an idea of engagement with your content and is the basis for conversion opportunities. A single visitor may visit multiple pages, so we also want to count the total number of users. We specifically want to measure this for organic traffic as it relates to our goal of growing organic traffic and increasing conversion rates. The goal is to grow your page views between 10% every 90 days and 25% on an annualized basis, the same as with impressions.

6. TIME ON SITE

Time that users spend on site can indicate whether the content they are viewing is engaging. When a site like Google ranks pages for relevance, one factor taken into account is the average time that organic traffic users spend looking at a specific page. When this number is high, rankings will improve and provide you with more visibility. While it's not always necessary to monitor each page individually, using page type categories (landing pages, blog posts, homepage) is helpful. To improve the time that users spend on your site, ensure that content is compelling, include relevant images, and provide more information.

7. BOUNCE RATE

A site's bounce rate is typically measured in two ways: categorizing the number of visitors that exit a site without viewing more than one page or those that spend a very short amount of time on the site overall. The overall goal is to lower bounce rate, which means retaining site visitors, but the threshold for what indicates a 'good' score can differ depending on the industry your page is tailored to and what type of page it is. To improve this score, working on individual pages or categorical content is recommended. Still, it's important to understand that higher percentages (between 45% and 55%) are considered typical and can only be improved over time.

8. USERS

	Acquisition		
Default Channel Grouping	Sessions ? ↓	% New Sessions ?	New Users ?
All Users	71,274 % of Total: 100.00% (71,274)	79.82% Avg for View: 79.82% (0.00%)	56,889 % of Total: 100.00% (56,889)
Organic Traffic	21,231 % of Total: 29.79% (71,274)	75.05% Avg for View: 79.82% (-5.98%)	15,933 % of Total: 28.01% (56,889)

Users are defined as "the total number of visitors for the requested time period." We want to measure this so that we know if we're growing the number of people going to the site – specifically the number visiting our target pages. The goal is to grow your user count between 10% every 90 days and 25% on an annualized basis.

9. CONVERSION RATE

375	172	547	$35,119.17	$328,200.00	934.53%
Total Forms	Total Calls	Total Conversions	Total Cost	Estimated Revenue	ROI

Your conversion rate is the percentage of users that visit your website relative to the number of conversions you have. On a target page level, this should be around 3%. It can sometimes be hard to measure this metric site-wide if your site contains a lot of educational content designed for a broad audience to consume. This is most likely to be an issue for local service businesses. By focusing on the target URLs in your campaign designed to convert, you can better manage your overall conversion rates in a matter that creates greater business success for your individual needs.

10. CONVERSIONS

Measuring the number of conversions is no different than checking to see how much money is in your bank account. All other metrics only exist to support this final – and very important – KPI. Conversions can be categorized as monetized engagement like calls, form submissions, a chat session, download into a funnel, and many more.

Each target page you're working on should have a conversion path or call to action that you can measure and monetize.

DIGITAL MARKETING KEY PERFORMANCE INDICATOR SUMMARY

We'll end where we started by saying: **You can't improve what you don't measure.** Before you apply any effort into a marketing campaign, you must have a base of accurate data to work with. Use the above KPIs to take control of your marketing initiatives, and you'll find that greater ROI is much easier to capture.

A good place to start is to find a group of marketing professionals willing and able to help you create and realize the right goals and objectives.

CHAPTER 4 REVIEW

1.   What key data points do you need to track to measure success?

GATHERING DATA

I will start this chapter by saying again: **You can't track what you don't measure**. I want to repeat this because it is one of the most important takeaways of this book.

In the previous chapter, we let you know what you need to track. Now, we will tell you how to measure that. This chapter provides an overview of what you need to track, and at the end of the book, you will find step-by-step guides that will walk you through exactly how to set up each platform. Below is the list of our core KPIs and the data platform you need to set up to track the necessary data.

Average Rank	Agency Analytics (or similar rank tracker)
Visibility Score	Agency Analytics (or similar rank tracker)
Impressions	Google Search Console
CTR	Google Search Console
Page Views	Google Analytics
Time on Site	Google Analytics
Bounce Rate	Google Analytics
Users	Google Analytics
Conversion Rate	Google Analytics
Conversion	Google Analytics and Call Tracking Metrics (if applicable)

You can choose to manage the data yourself by logging into each tool and exporting your data to a spreadsheet. Or you can use a tool like Google Data Studio to create integrations to manage most of your data. If you're looking for a simpler process, I recommend checking out AgencyAnalytics.com. They provide an easy-to-use dashboard that takes care of all of this for you.

CHAPTER 5 REVIEW

1. What tools will you need to capture your data?

2. Will you use a third-party platform, or will you manage the data yourself?

CHAPTER 6

START WHERE YOU ARE

Before we start the process, we need to discuss one important strategy that will determine your ultimate level of success by saving you time and money (maybe even your sanity).

The first goal of SEO is to rank your site for specific keywords. To do that, you'll need to know what your current ranks tell you about where you are in your journey. Yes, this book will be packed with strategies to walk you through every step needed to be successful, BUT what if you didn't need to do all of the steps? What if you could laser target your efforts on the exact strategy you need today to beat your competitors? Would that save you time and money? The answer, of course, is YES!

HOW DO WE KNOW WHERE TO START THEN?

Your current ranks tell you a lot about what needs to be done. To organize this, I created four buckets of current ranks. This process has worked for me well over the past decade and continues to get fast results for my clients. The four buckets are:

Bucket #4: Not Ranking
Bucket #3: Traction
Bucket #2: First Page
Bucket #1: Top 3

WHAT DO THESE BUCKETS MEAN FOR YOU?

The simple answer... Everything. By first looking at where your site is sitting, you can dive right into the optimization strategy that best fits your needs today. Then, over time as things improve (when you follow the steps in this book), you can review your current positions and use them as a guide for what you need to be doing today.

Below is a preview of the strategy behind each rank. Follow along with these as you read future chapters to see how this all ties back to generating traffic fast and growing your campaign month after month.

BUCKET #4: NOT RANKING

We consider any keyword with a rank over 50 as having a 'not ranking' status.

So, what if none of your keywords are ranking? What do you do? The best bet is to start with onsite work and branding. If you think driving links will help, you're in for a world of trouble. If your site is indexed properly, has no major technical issues, has decent content, and you've correctly submitted your site to the search engines, then you will rank for something. It might not be a lot, but it'll be something.

If you're seeing nothing… onsite and branding is where to start.

BUCKET #3: TRACTION

We consider any keyword with a rank of 11-50 to have 'traction.'

Traction means the search engines have acknowledged your site and its content and are giving you as much credit as they're willing to provide you with currently. To improve from here, you'll use a combination of competitive analysis and link building. Each of these topics is a chapter later in the book.

BUCKET #2: FIRST PAGE

We consider any keyword with a rank of 4-10 to be on the 'first page' but not yet where we want them to be.

To get to this point, you must have great content, a technically sound website, proper mobile optimization, great branding, and a few authority links to your site. While being on the first page is great, it still doesn't help ring the register, so we need to move into the top three spots.

BUCKET #1: TOP 3

We consider any keyword with a rank of 1-3 as being in the 'top 3.' Now there are a lot of variables to this. Local Maps rankings will push the top organic spot to #4. If you're working on a national campaign, the way you measure Top 3 will be different than how you measure a local campaign. The same is true for featured snippets, which some people consider spot 0 (better than 1).

Often in local, this can be a simple matter of reviews (a chapter on reviews is included). In hyper-competitive markets, you may need to be looking at the quality and quantity of links coming to your site. To dominate and control the top spots for competitive keywords, you need to hit home on the majority of your Key Performance Indicators (KPI) – this is a book on Local SEO, so we'll cover all of those as well.

With SEO, there is an 80/20 rule, meaning 80% of the time, these rules will ring true. There are cases where people can violate these rules to manipulate a search result using only Latin copy, but what does that prove? If you can't make money off the traffic you're driving, then what is the point? We've got a chapter on that as well.

Let's move onto an overview of running a campaign. Each item in the overview will have an associated chapter diving deeper into the topic.

My main goal for you, the reader, is to understand you DO NOT have to do everything in the book to win. You have to determine where you are today using our data-driven approach and then work only on the things most likely to benefit you today. Everything else can wait.

Section 3 –
The Strategies

CHAPTER 7

Google My Business (GMB)

Author: Mark Luckenbaugh - Local Viking

Google Local Ranking Factors: Explanation and Action Plan

Many factors affect your rank in local search results, but some matter to Google way more than others. The good news is that we can break the algorithm down into three main pillars: prominence, relevance, and proximity.

All local ranking factors fall into at least one of these categories. We'll take a deep dive into the most important factors under each pillar to help you understand how Google decides rankings. Even better, we've also included a concrete action plan that will help you optimize your content, build a more visible online brand, and snatch those top local pack positions.

THE THREE PILLARS OF LOCAL SEO

1. PROMINENCE

If you're familiar with organic SEO's E-A-T pillars (Expertise, Authority, Trust), you can think of "prominence" as local SEO's counterpart to "authority." Prominence refers to how popular or well-known your business is to its users. The more prominent you are, the more likely you'll rank in the local search results.

Your prominence is affected by online and offline factors. If you are prominent in the real world, then search results will reflect that as well. Google also considers your brand visibility online – more citations, links, features, and positive reviews boost your prominence.

2. RELEVANCE

Relevance is the foundation of not just SEO but Google's entire algorithm. When a user searches for a specific keyword, Google wants to give them the most relevant and useful results that match their query. For example, a digital marketing agency listing wouldn't be very relevant to someone looking for a place to eat.

Increasing your relevance is simple enough. You must optimize your content and other related entities so that Google understands what your business is all about. You can do this by completing your online profiles and adding relevant keywords.

3. PROXIMITY

Proximity is about how close your business is to the user. For example, suppose someone is searching "best pizza restaurants" in New York. In that case, Google won't return results in California unless the user includes a location keyword in their search term (e.g., "best pizza restaurants San Diego").

Google's algorithm for proximity is more complex than most people realize. Your search term and location play a role, of course, but there are other factors involved as well. If you are walking and search for "pizza near me," for example, Google will show you restaurants that are within walking distance rather than those that require a drive or commute.

Distance is a significant factor in local SEO because a user is more likely to patronize a closer business. This is also an interesting pillar to work with because it's a bit more challenging to influence compared to relevance and prominence.

Since you cannot move your business address to rank in other locations, you have to optimize your local business profile to display your business to the customers you want to reach. Conventional rank trackers are notoriously inaccurate because Google serves results based on the user's location, and that varies wildly from user to user and even device to device.

How to Rank Locally in Google

So how can you use your knowledge of prominence, relevance, and proximity to influence your rankings?

The trick is to create an action plan that specifically targets each of the pillars. You need to have all three to rank high – focusing on just one or two won't cut it. You don't have to put equal effort into all three; you can push harder on a specific factor you lack as long as all three are present.

Keep reading for hard-hitting, actionable optimization tactics for better local rankings.

INCREASING YOUR PROMINENCE

Building prominence is all about building brand reputation and awareness. In this section, we'll cover some of the most impactful prominence-building tactics: social media, link building, and reviews.

ESTABLISH SOCIAL MEDIA PROFILES

It might sound very basic, but you'd be surprised at how many businesses don't get this step right. If you want to do SEO – heck, if you're going to do any business – you must have your social media profiles fully fleshed out.

Categorize each social media platform into essential social profiles and secondary profiles. Essential profiles include the major social media networks like Facebook, Instagram, LinkedIn, Twitter, and other industry-specific platforms (e.g., Yelp, Trip Advisor, etc.). Set these up first, and once you've established your essential profiles, you can move on to lesser-known secondary sites like Academia.edu or Square Cash.

BUILD CITATIONS

General citation building is not as impactful as it used to be but having a strong backlink profile is still an important ranking factor. If your citations are properly done, they can help move the needle of your local rankings.

The first thing to consider is that low-quality directory listings will not likely maintain a decent index rate. Keep this in mind when considering using duplicate content or not filling out the listings completely.

Step One: Build your top citations—also known as your Top 50 Citations. This list is one of the many resources inside our Local SEO Toolbox that you can download for free. These more authoritative directories should be your first wave of citations on every new site.

Step Two: Compose a list and start building your niche-relevant and geo-specific citations. These fall between the cracks of the citation building conversation far too often but can actually move the needle—big time. In some cases, you will incur a fee to list your website on these directories, but I believe it is money well spent on links that will be highly relevant to your money site.

Step Three: Reverse engineering competitors will forever be one of my most favorite ways of building a customized rankings strategy for each new site for which we are building a campaign. There is no difference with citations. Using Whitespark to mine citation opportunities is a no-brainer. Once you or your team compiles this list, you can start building based on the specs below. Easy as pie.

Step Four: Build your supporting citations. These buggers are cheap, and you can build them fast. The build specs listed below should apply, but you could still run into some of the same indexation issues as poorly built citations due to the lower quality of some of the platforms, which is something to consider.

REINFORCE YOUR BACKLINK PROFILE

Linking to your "properties" can pass link juice. Take advantage of this by creating a backlink graph or a list/collection of your most important backlinks. Adding this to your website comes with plenty of benefits:

- Encourages faster indexing since Google can just crawl that page for new links.

- Adds authority/prominence signals because you have several sites linking back to you.

- Adds relevance signals because Google takes each citation in context. This means that they look at who is linking to you, what type of site they are, the content your link was placed in, the link's anchor text, and many other factors, to determine the "topic" of your site/page.

COLLECT REVIEWS

Reviews are a controversial aspect of local SEO – some experts say they matter while others say they don't. Our tests show that most businesses should see a minimal increase in rankings thanks to re-view generation campaigns. While reviews are important, they shouldn't be the end-all-be-all of your SEO strategy.

Aside from rankings, there are many ways that reviews can help your business. More positive reviews increase trust and prominence with Google, even if they are hosted on a third-party platform. Higher ratings also develop trust with potential customers, putting you in a more advantageous position than lower-rated competitors.

How to Collect Reviews

Before generating reviews for your business, decide where you will do it. The most common places to generate reviews are on your Google My Business listing, Facebook Business Page, and Yelp pro-file. Some businesses have niche-specific sites worth having reviews placed on, such as HealthGrades.com for doctors and Lawyer.com for lawyers.

Once you determine which business profiles you will generate reviews for, you will need a software system that can automate sending text messages and emails inviting your customers to leave feedback for you online. The review generation software space is filled with tools that you can set and forget, such as BirdEye, Rep.co, and Podium.

With your chosen tool, you'll be able to set up review request campaigns that can sync with your CRM or customer list and ensure that a steady stream of reviews comes to your chosen profiles.

INCREASING YOUR RELEVANCE

When trying to improve your relevance score, there are two things to keep in mind: your location and your niche. In this section, we'll look at adding niche and geographical keywords to help in-crease your relevance.

OPTIMIZE YOUR GMB CONTENT

If you aren't optimizing your GMB content for relevant keywords, then you're losing out on a lot of relevance. Don't over-optimize by stuffing your listing with keywords – that's the best way to get penalized by Google.

Make sure that your content contains the right keywords while still being natural and easy to read. Use synonyms, related search terms, and LSI keywords. You can also use a tool to generate keywords and calculate ideal keyword density so that your content is on par with your competition.

CHOOSE THE RIGHT CATEGORY

The category that you choose on GMB can significantly impact the search terms for which you rank. Choose the most specific and most accurate category possible.

ADD GEO MARKERS

Increase your geo-identifiers or other information that specifies your location, including zip codes, neighborhoods, GPS coordinates, Maps pin location, and more. The more of these you have, the stronger your geographical relevance.

OPTIMIZE YOUR WEBSITE'S LOCATION PAGE

Although organic SEO is a completely separate field, it synergizes with your local SEO efforts. Google looks at your organic rankings to help determine your local search rankings, so it's important to keep your website optimized for niche and location keywords. You can add a location page to your well-ranking website to boost your local performance.

OPTIMIZE YOUR PHOTO & VIDEO CONTENT

Optimizing your visual content is a small yet impactful step you can take to get better local rankings. Photo/video optimization covers a wide range of practices, from choosing the best images/ videos to adding alt text to compressing file sizes to improve page speed.

CONNECT RELATED ENTITIES

Connect your online brand entities such as your website, GMB profile, social media profiles, and more. Creating an interlinked network of pages is a great way to build relevance and authority in Google's eyes. Plus, linking out to your profiles can encourage users to learn more about what you do and further engage with your brand.

INCREASING YOUR PROXIMITY

As we mentioned earlier, working with proximity is tricky. We have conducted many tests and experiments to see what works to increase proximity signals, and we've compiled our findings into our 50-minute GMB State of the Union video. Watch the video to learn more about effective proximity-building strategies at LocalViking.com/GMB-Training-Webinar.

OTHER HELPFUL RANKING TIPS

With your foundational ranking strategy in place, you should make sure that you are giving your business the edge against your competition by looking at the following areas.

YOUTUBE CHANNEL

Creating video content and using it on your YouTube Channel and website is a great way to interact with potential customers on a personal level and increase online traffic and activity across your digital properties.

Don't forget to use keyword-rich playlist titles and link from your channel and videos back to your website and GMB profile (and vice versa).

REPORT AND REMOVE SPAM

Spam listings have plagued Google Maps, and as a result, Google has given you the tools to remove or reduce the effectiveness of spam listings in your local market.

To fight spam, search for your product or service on Google and analyze the listings you see that rank above your business. Are any obviously fake listings? Use the Google Maps interface to 'suggest an edit' to any fake listings and mark them as closed.

Sometimes competitors break Google's GMB naming terms of service so that they can 'stuff' target keywords into the title of their GMB listing. If you see competitors doing this, simply use the same 'suggest an edit' interface on Google Maps and correct the name of the listing to the business entity's legal name.

IMPORTANT SECONDARY LISTINGS

As we mentioned earlier in this chapter, getting citations or listings on commonly used business profiles is an important aspect of local SEO. As you take stock of where your business is listed online, double-check that you have taken care of all of the following profiles.

1. BING PLACES

Importing your GMB listing into Bing maps is as simple as logging into Bing Places and clicking the 'import' button. Once your listing is live, your business will show up in local results in the default Internet Explorer search engine.

2. APPLE MAPS

Adding a business to Apple maps can be done manually. As soon as your business is listed, it will show up on the native Maps application for all iOS devices.

3. LOCAL CHAMBER OF COMMERCE

Links from relevant and authoritative sources are great for your rankings, and your local Chamber of Commerce website usually satisfies all of the requirements for a great local link.

4. GPS PLATFORMS

TomTom, Waze, and other platforms contributing to the GPS and direction ecosystem keep their own business and location information in which your business data can be included.

5. GEO SPECIFIC

Some web directories and business listing websites are geographically oriented. If your business qualifies, it's usually not a bad idea to get listed there. Think about a website specifically for listing places and businesses in the specific county where your business resides.

6. NICHE SPECIFIC

Industry or vertical-specific sites are plentiful these days. We recommend taking the time to build a list of niche-specific sites on which you may be able to list your business.

CONCLUSION

Your local ranking is based on a complex web of factors. It's important to know which ones affect your rankings the most and which are a waste of resources. Focus on building your prominence, relevance, and proximity through our concrete action plan steps, and you'll see your online brand grow in no time.

We appreciate Mark's in-depth overview a ton! Here is a step-by-step guide to setting up your GMB from the team at Enfusen.

How to Setup a Google My Business Listing

1. You must have a Gmail account to set up a Google My Business listing. We recommend using a Gmail that is associated with your company name.

   Example:
   Company Name: Enfusen Digital Marketing
   Gmail: enfusen@gmail.com

2. Once you have your Gmail account set up, create a Google My Business account at www.Google.com/Business/.

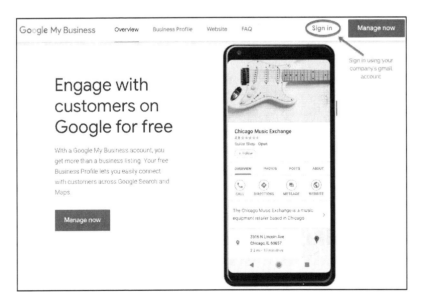

3. Enter the following business information

   • Business Name
   • Business Category

- Business Location

4. Click submit. Google will notify you that you will receive a postcard with a code at your business location within two weeks to verify your listing. Once you receive the postcard, go to your Google My Business listing and enter in the code to be officially verified.

5. You can view your GMB account at any time by clicking on the square to the left of your Google icon and clicking on the blue business icon.

6. Once you have a verified GMB account, we recommend adding as much business information as possible to increase the value, including:

- Photos of your office building, team, products/services
- Business short name
- Services that you offer
- Business hours
- Service areas
- Website URL
- Business description

CHAPTER 7 REVIEW

1. Have you set up your GMB?

2. Is your GMB fully optimized based on the best practices listed in this chapter?

3. Did you sign up for LocalViking.com?

CHAPTER 8

COMPETITIVE ANALYSIS

Author: Roger Bryan - Growth Foundry

Many people believe that the goal of Local SEO is to beat Google, which can be true to some degree, but you are really trying to beat your competitors. Our team learned early on that to improve your rank in local marketing, you only need to do a little better than your competition from a local SEO perspective.

This chapter is designed to help you understand how to look at your competitor's website from a marketing lens and includes action steps you need to take to run a proper competitive analysis and outlines the necessary tasks that need to be completed to beat them.

To begin your competitive analysis, go to SEMRush.com. Type the URL of the page you are trying to optimize into the search bar and look at the following Keywords. Search by highest volume and then by highest CPC. Find 5-10 core keywords that have high search volume or CPC that you could rank your page for. Also, try to find the keywords the page is currently ranking or gaining traction for. It is much easier to rank a page for keywords already ranking than with no rank.

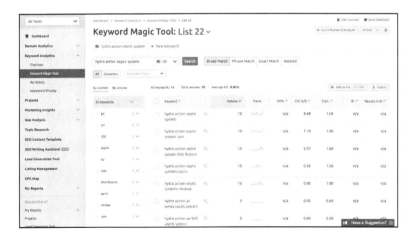

Get our experts to do all the work - https://growthfoundry.com/rank-me

COMPETITORS

Review profiles of your competitors to see if they are running paid advertising. If so, what kind? For example, AdWords, Bing, Remarketing, etc.

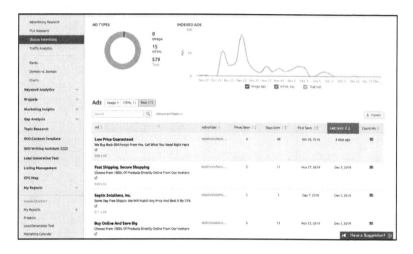

- Which of the following pages do they have rankings on?
  - o Home page
  - o Service page
  - o FAQ page
  - o Blog post
- What keywords are they ranking for?
- What keywords is that page ranking for that you need to beat them for?
- What does the page look like?
- How many images?
- Is there a video?
- Is there rich media?

Open an incognito window for Google search and type in the primary keyword.

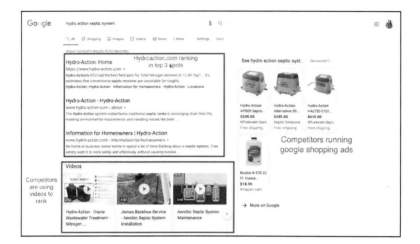

Create a list of all competitors' websites ranking above you. Look specifically at the website URL. Is it a home page, service page, or FAQ page? This matters. Create a list of what is on their website, such as:

- Images
- Photos
- Videos
- PDF downloads
- Internal links
- Headers
- Core keywords
- FAQ section
- Type of content

Example: Do they have something unique like a list of all counties they service with links? Do they list all services with the location to rank better for all areas? What could you duplicate?

Next, look at the "people also ask" at the bottom of the page to find other keywords that people search to find you.

Searches related to hydro action septic system

hydro action septic system **distributors**   hydro action **distributor**

hydro action **ap 500 alarm**   **aerobic treatment unit cost**

septic system **manufacturers**   **hydroaction atu**

fiberglass aerobic septic **tank**   septic **solutions**

1 2 3 4 5 6 7 8 9 10   Next

Run the page through PageOptimizer.pro, which will provide a full list of recommendations for you to implement on your landing page to beat out your competition.

HOW TO USE PAGE OPTIMIZER PRO

1. Login and click the blue button labeled "New Project"

2. Enter in the URL of the page you are trying to optimize

3. Download the POP chrome extension

4. Name the project (Example: Aeration Septic – Septic Tank Inspection)

5. Click the orange button labeled "New Page"

6. Choose the POP full report

7. Add in the main keyword

   Examples: Hydro action septic system, Septic Tank Inspection, Concrete Septic Tank

8. Do not choose any of the special options, just scroll down to next. Then, POP will find your current organic competitors

9. Go through the list and choose your top competition that POP pulls

10. Add any additional keywords you want to use

11. Run the full report.

    It normally takes some time to crawl and populate the report. I recommend running it the day before you would like to analyze it.

12. Review the POP analysis

13. Click "Dashboard"

14. Go to the second tab titled "Recommendations" and review everything POP is recommending.

15. Add each recommendation as a task in Asana

CHAPTER 8 REVIEW

1. Who are the top three competitors you need to outrank?

2. What are the key metrics you've found that you will focus on when launching your campaign?

CHAPTER 9

Rank for Your Brand First

Author: Roger Bryan - Growth Foundry

Start at the Beginning When Building Your Brand

When you begin creating an SEO strategy for your business, you may be unsure of the correct first step to take.

Do you start by having a great deal of content? Begin the process of getting your products or services out to the public? Start a social media page? All of these aspects are important, and when you approach it from the right angle, they will all work together to help you succeed.

Gaining organic traffic for new brands seems daunting, but it doesn't need to be if you follow one simple step.

Build Your Brand and Make it Solid

Today, it seems like there's a way to connect with your audience no matter how you want to do it.

Twitter allows you to post short, to-the-point updates.

Facebook allows your business to post pictures and products, connecting directly to your audience.

Instagram focuses on sharing products and services via images.

LinkedIn allows you to focus on your history and connections to increase your reputation.

But are all of these platforms necessary for successful businesses? The short answer is yes, but only if you can do it in a cohesive, consistent manner.

When you build your brand, you're focused on getting your message out to the right audience. This needs to be done in a way that makes sense for your business, and in a way that will last. Read on to find out more about using social media to your advantage as a way to build your brand and increase traffic and lead conversion over time.

WHERE TO START WHEN IT COMES TO BRAND BUILDING

1. USE THE SAME NAME

The first step is claiming the same name across all social media profiles. This allows your customers – and potential customers – to find you easily, no matter what platform they use. It's also a great idea to use the same profile picture in your header. There's an opportunity for creativity with the updates you make, but your page should be set up to reflect the same tone across the board.

2. PROVIDE THE SAME INFORMATION

This doesn't mean make the same updates on every social media page or platform. Instead, provide consistent contact information for your business. The following are necessary to ensure your customers have direct access to you and your business whenever they need it, even if they're checking out a new platform or page for the first time.

- Name
- Address
- Phone number/numbers
- Social media account links

Don't Be Afraid to Post to or Share These Pages!

The point of creating different social media pages to build your brand is to *use* them. Post to each of them regularly. It doesn't have to be daily but having weekly or twice weekly posts is a great way to increase visibility, generate content, and begin to use the pages and profiles to your advantage.

Remember: The more content you have on these pages, the more likely potential customers will engage with them. From there, these leads will follow links to your website, blog, or even to your other social media pages. The goal is to keep people invested, and this happens when the content is new, exciting, and engaging.

Use your *other* social media pages and your website to advertise the individual links. If someone visits your Instagram, direct them to Twitter for pointed, timely updates, or to Facebook to connect with other clients, customers, and visitors. It's all connected – and it's **meant** to be. Build your brand by building a network – it works!

SEO is All About the Ranking

For startups and new small businesses, the goal is for your name – your *brand* – to appear on the first page of search engines like Google. The more relevant pages you create, the better the odds are that this will happen.

For many businesses, the first results that show up during a search are social media pages. This might seem counterproductive because you need people to visit your *main* site to convert them, but it's actually the opposite.

Use the appearance of your social media pages in search engine results to your advantage.

Before visitors ever click on the link to your site, they'll often go to your social media pages. This is great exposure for your business and your brand, but it's also an excellent way for these visitors to get a feel for your company as a whole.

Create attractive content of varied types – but make it *consistent.* One of the most critical steps you should take while building your brand is to establish a consistent tone of voice. This doesn't mean using the *same* content across the board, but brand confidence is built when customers know what to expect – and it *lasts* when people like what they see.

BUILD BRAND AUTHORITY BY USING EVERY PLATFORM

Brand authority results from numerous backlinks (links that redirect visitors from one social media site or post to your website). The more traffic you have, the better. This seems like common sense, right? But knowing how to use each platform to increase visitor engagement (likes, comments, reposts, shares) takes some thought – and careful planning.

There are plenty of different social media platforms to use, but the following five are some of the most useful for building your brand and establishing brand authority through engagement.

LinkedIn: The ideal networking site for companies because it connects you to other businesses and industry leaders. Recommendations and endorsements through this site say a great deal about your business status and potential. LinkedIn allows you to make connections, post updates, and use searchable hashtags.

YouTube: Creating a video channel gives you a chance to brand build in a hands-on way. Via this platform, leads see and hear you speak, and they can familiarize themselves with your products and services. This is a chance for you to be truly creative with the titles you choose for your videos, as well as the style you choose to film them. When people search for something on YouTube, their eyes are drawn to two things: exciting thumbnails and view numbers.

Facebook: Allows you to build a community via "friend" posts, comments, and reviews, and then cross-post content from your other platforms, too. Facebook's new updates make it possible to search for keywords, filter through reviews, and engage with the people who have the loudest voices, be it through reviews, shares, or overall interaction. Positivity on Facebook goes a long way.

Twitter: The ideal place to come up with the *perfect* hashtag, Twitter posts are meant to be brief. This is an excellent opportunity to write short, snappy updates and include links, graphics, and animated gifs – all relevant to your brand, of course. Twitter's reach is endless, especially for those who take advantage.

Instagram: This platform allows you to include links in your bio, place direct links within posts to products for sale, connect with other companies, *and* interact with your customers and followers. Mostly visual in nature, Instagram's algorithm promotes more successful posts. So, the more likes and comments you get, the better your chances are of being seen – and trusted! Like Twitter, Facebook, and LinkedIn, using the right hashtags is essential, and another **great** way to establish consistency.

CHAPTER 9 REVIEW

1. Do you have all of your needed social media profiles set up?

2. What 10 assets do you plan on ranking on the first page of Google to control your brand?

CHAPTER 10

Picking the Right Keywords

Author: Roger Bryan - Growth Foundry

You should already be doing proper keyword research if you're trying to expand your reach on Google. Your goal is to improve your rankings and get more eyes on your business. To do that, you must use proper keywords, but knowing which keywords to choose can seem like a daunting task. You're a businessperson, not an online marketer. Still, if you're unsure which keywords to use in your marketing, you won't rank as high.

Search engines like Google are built to be consumer-friendly, and don't have businesses in mind. Instead, they want to provide a service to the average, everyday person who goes to Google to look something up, such as a list of all the pizza places or dentists near them. To do that, they'll type in a single word or even an entire phrase.

Your goal is to find out what keyword(s) or phrases they'll use. If you choose the right ones and have the right content, your business will be featured over other businesses whose keywords aren't as optimized. Throughout your website content, blogs, etc., you should use your targeted keywords so that it comes up when someone does a search using the keywords you chose. Doing this speeds up the time in which people find your website, improving your overall rankings.

Finding the Right Keywords

Hopefully, before you even think about doing keyword research, you've created a buyer persona for your company. This makes finding your keywords easier because it allows you to understand who is buying from you. It will give you a good glimpse of their buying habits and what it takes to get them to your site. Once you have all this figured out, then you move on to the next step: **brainstorming**.

Really think about your buyer persona. What are their interests? Are they a targeted consumer group or your everyday average buyers? For example, if you sell diapers, then you want to target parents. Targeting everyone with a broad stroke is a waste of time and advertising dollars. Finding the right buyers interested in your products is key moving forward. During this brainstorming session, you need to sit down and think about ten words associated with the buyer persona.

Again, using "diapers" as an example, make a list of ten words you can think of that a parent would type into Google search. Then, come up with phrases that might accompany those words. "Where can I buy diapers near me?" is a good example. If you're unsure, you can use Google to help you out. Type in the keyword and at the bottom of the screen, Google will share a list of related searches.

By getting to know your buyer persona, what they search for, and how they write their search phrases, you're well on your way to improving your keywords and ranking on Google.

Using Google Ads to Test a Keyword Strategy

If you are running a paid advertising campaign, you should use this strategy to your advantage. You have search terms and data within your campaign that show what keywords are performing best for your paid campaigns. This can be extremely relevant when choosing your organic keyword strategy.

First, review the search terms over the past 90 days to see if any search terms have converted. Next, review the keywords inside your campaign and filter by conversion rate to know which keywords your audience is resonating with most. For more information on using paid traffic to build your keyword, list read our blog post about it at https://www.rcbryan.com/how-do-you-know-youve-chosen-the-right-keywords-for-your-campaign.

Chapter 10 Review

1. What are the top five keywords that you will be targeting?
2. What are the landing pages associated with each keyword?

CHAPTER 11

On Page Optimization

Author: Roger Bryan - Growth Foundry

How to Optimize Your Blog Post for Rank, Traffic, and Conversion

As a business owner, having powerful content for your customers to engage with your brand is an important part of your online presence and the relationships with your customers. This step-by-step guide will help you create, write, and optimize your blog content to drive more traffic and increase conversion.

Using the following 14 strategies, you can turn your average blog post into a piece of important content on your company's site that will drive your customers to convert.

1. Finding the right topic ideas
2. Planning your post around important keywords
3. Understanding what your customer is looking for
4. How to focus on the introduction
5. Writing memorable headlines
6. Optimizing your headings
7. How to optimize your title tag and meta descriptions
8. Choosing tags and categories properly
9. How to use opening loops
10. What easter eggs are and how to hide them
11. What images to include
12. How to beat your competitors in blog content
13. Different types of rich media you can use
14. How to structure your content

1. FINDING TOPIC IDEAS

Not having ideas for blog posts can slow down the content creation process. There are a variety of places you can look to find the right topics.

Quora: Go to Quora and search your key term (for example, "physical therapy") to find a list of commonly asked questions that people need answers to. Use those questions to craft blog post topics.

Google: Go to Google and type in your primary keyword to see if there are featured snippets or frequently asked questions that could be used as the base for your blog post

Buzzsumo: Visit this site to find viral content. You can choose specific articles, content, or infographics that you see are already working and put it in your posts.

Competitors: Look at what your competitors are writing about and see if you can use it as inspiration.

Google Trends (Trends.Google.com/Trends/Explore): allows you to see what the world is searching for and what is trending. You can search for specific topics like physical therapy to see the most common topics people are searching for.

Google News: Provides current news that allows you to stay relevant within your industry. This is a great resource to search for current news in your industry and be one of the first to write about it.

Related Terms (bottom of Google Search): After searching for key terms on Google, you can scroll down to the bottom of the page where you will find "related search terms." This is a great place to find similar topics that people are also searching for.

Searches related to physical therapy

cleveland clinic physical therapy
physical therapy **salary**
physical therapy **near me**
cleveland clinic physical therapy **strongsville**
physical therapy **education**
university hospital outpatient physical therapy
uh physical therapy **near me**
physical therapy **exercises**

1 2 3 4 5 6 7 8 9 10   Next

2. PLANNING YOUR POST AROUND IMPORTANT KEYWORDS

Determining what keywords you should be writing your post around is the most important aspect of content creation. A few great places to determine what keywords you should be using include:

1. Keywords your competitors are ranking for and writing about

2. Google searches that tell you what others are frequently asking

3. Featured snippets or Google questions for this topic

4. If you are trying to rank a specific landing page, use keywords that page is centered around

5. Keywords are you trying to rank for that are related to the post topics

EXAMPLE OF A FEATURED SNIPPET

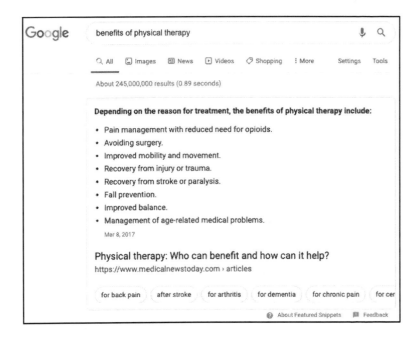

3. UNDERSTAND WHAT YOUR CUSTOMER IS LOOKING FOR

Use search console, Google analytics, and other data research to see what words people are searching for to find an answer to their question. You want to optimize your blog post for the problems in which they are trying to find the solution. You also want to meet the customer where they are in the buyer's journey. Whether it is a brand-new customer who has never heard of you before or someone already familiar with your brand, you want to make sure the content you present to them is relevant. A strategy you can use to create content made for your buyers' journey is TOFU, MOFU, BOFU.

TOFU (TOP OF FUNNEL)

- Building awareness about your services/the problem you address
- Blog posts
- eBooks

MOFU (MIDDLE OF FUNNEL)

- Teaching your customers how to choose a solution
- Case Studies
- eBooks
- White papers
- Webinars or Podcasts
- Video tutorials

BOFU (BOTTOM OF FUNNEL)

- Explaining why your product is the best solution
- Free trial
- Free consultation
- Urgency Offers

4. FOCUS ON THE INTRODUCTION

The initial sentence should be short, punchy, and create lots of curiosity. Remember, you only have 2.7 seconds to grab your customer's attention before they click off your page. Out of all the content they view every day, make sure yours stands out from the crowd, and the intro is the most important part.

Five classic ways to open a blog:

1. Start with a question from a reader

If your blog post answers a question from a reader, make sure to start with the question that could be answered by reading.

2. The success story

Pull the reader in by telling how someone solved their problem with your solution.

Example: The success of physical therapy on a specific type of injury

3. **The what if**

Paint the story to the reader of the "what if" situation.

Example: "What if physical therapy could take away your chronic pain without medication?"

4. **The pain vs. gain**

Start by building up pain and empathy that your audience can relate to. The more you build the story, the more compelled the reader is to continue with the article.

5. **The exchange**

Start by telling the reader the exact benefit they will receive in exchange for what you are offering. Then provide the solution by promising the benefit in exchange for reading.

5. WRITE MEMORABLE HEADLINES

The title should always contain the primary keyword. Headlines should make the reader "have to read the rest" This is similar to your introduction. You want to make sure that when the reader sees your headline, they want to continue reading the first paragraph. When writing headlines, think about the following:

- Use the words that describe the topic in your blog title. Avoid ambiguity.

- Ask yourself, "If I were a member of my audience, why would I read this blog post instead of other similar posts? Why?" Then, like a little kid, go down the why rabbit hole to get to the core value you are providing to your readers.

- Just like you would with marketing a product, define the value proposition for your blog posts and include that in your blog titles.

EXAMPLES OF WELL WRITTEN BLOG POST TITLES

6. OPTIMIZE YOUR HEADINGS

Look for opportunities to (naturally) include your keywords in the page heading. That includes anything that has a <h1>, <h2>, or <h3> tag on the page. These special headings are larger than the normal text and tell Google that this is the subject of your post. See the image below for examples. Headings are often a good place to include similar core words that your blog post is about (see words highlighted in yellow as examples).

EXAMPLES OF HEADERS

\<H1\> or Primary Keyword: Winter Activity Injuries: What Can Happen to Those Who Aren't Careful Outdoors in the Cold
\<H2\>: Injuries while playing winter sports
\<H3\>: Who really likes winter weather?

EXAMPLES OF DIFFERENT HEADINGS:

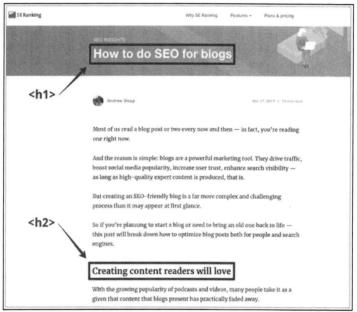

Image from SERanking.com/blog/header-tags/

USE RELEVANT INTERNAL LINKS

Each time you write a new post, think about blog posts you've previously published that are relevant to what you're writing now. Wherever it makes sense to do so, add in those links. If you can do it naturally, use anchor text that relates to your target keyword for the older post you're linking to. Another part of internal linking is driving your reader to convert on your website. Add a call-to-action link that drives the customer to a landing page where they can schedule an appointment.

1. OPTIMIZE YOUR TITLE TAG AND META DESCRIPTION

Make sure to use your target keyword in your title tag and meta description. Your title tag and meta description are displayed when your web page is displayed on Google. The goal of your title and description is to motivate someone who finds your page in a Google search to click on your link, which drives them to your website. To get people to click through to your page, make sure your meta description has a clear call to action or tells how you are solving their problem. Make a compelling offer that is different from your competitor's title and description and will make them click to your page.

Your title tag should be 50-60 characters long, and the meta description should be 50-160 characters. Sometimes, Google does not show the entire meta description in searches, so ensure that the first three lines include the most important information that will make a reader click to read your blog post. These sentences will tell the reader what your post is about, and, if it relates to what they need, make them click on it.

Physical therapy: Who can benefit and how can it help? **Title Tag**
https://www.medicalnewstoday.com › articles ▾
Mar 8, 2017 - Depending on the reason for treatment, the **benefits of physical therapy** include: Pain management with reduced need for opioids. Avoiding surgery. Improved mobility and movement. Recovery from injury or trauma. Recovery from stroke or paralysis. Fall prevention. Improved balance. Management of age-related medical ...
Meta Description

2. CHOOSE TAGS AND CATEGORIES PROPERLY

Blogs allow you to create tags and categories that help you group related posts. This is a useful navigational aid for people browsing your blog and a tool you can use strategically for SEO. Every category or tag you use creates a new page that will include the name of the tag or category in the URL, and a lot of relevant content and links on the page.

3. OPENING LOOPS

Give a cliffhanger to the audience by opening loops in your blog posts that pose a question or point to more information later in the article.

Example: "As you'll see in just a second, you will become a pro at this industry." It makes the reader keep reading.

4. HIDE EASTER EGGS

An Easter Egg acts as an inside joke the target audience would bond to; something the reader doesn't need to understand but would make your target audience think the content was made specifically for them.

5. INCLUDE IMAGES

A good blog post should always have images associated. Images should have proper image alt tags and descriptions related to the keywords for which your blog post is trying to rank. Always use commercial use images in your posts and avoid using free stock images. Google looks for unique images that do not appear anywhere else on the web.

6. UNDERSTAND YOUR COMPETITION

If you are trying to outrank your competition for a specific blog post topic, make sure you are using more text and more images than they are. If your competition has 500 words, you should have at least 501 words.

7. USING RICH MEDIA

There are several different types of rich media you can add to your blog posts to increase the value it brings to your reader, including videos, infographics, GIFs, and Guides/PDFs.

8. Focus on the closing

You always want a call to action when closing your blog post that can drive readers closer to scheduling an appointment or learning about your business. Leave them wanting more. Linking to other posts that have a relevant topic is a great way to drive customers deeper into your site and providing value.

At the end of the blog post, make sure that you give the reader a summary of the entire post with the most important information you want them to retain. Then, end with a compelling ask that will attempt to drive the reader to schedule a consultation.

5 Examples of blog post closings

1. Close + Offer: Tie your closing to one of your offers and something the reader can do.

2. Ask for more input: This could be asking the writer to comment or share on social media

3. Tell people what to do now: Ask them to contact your office, schedule a meeting, fill out a form, or read another similar post

4. Ask for a response: Ask a specific question like, "When playing sports, what is your favorite PT exercise?"

5. Remind the readers of the original promise: Circling back to the beginning can help close the loop and help the reader feel like the blog post delivered on your promise.

Add Social Share Buttons

Make it easy for your customers to share your content. There are several plugins or tools you can use to add this functionality to your blog post easily and cost-effectively. One of our favorite plugins for social sharing is the https://warfareplugins.com/.

STRUCTURE THE CONTENT PROPERLY

Nobody wants to read a massive paragraph of text. The easier you make the blog post to read, the easier it will be for Google to read it. A few ways to structure your blog post is:

- Use headers with prominent keywords to break up paragraphs inside your blog post
- Include bullet points and numbered lists
- Bold and italicize important words you want your reader to find
- Make your paragraphs short and sweet

CHAPTER 11 REVIEW

1. Are all five of your target pages optimized using the above best practices?

"GET THE CLICK" — META OPTIMIZATION

Author: Roger Bryan - Growth Foundry

TITLE TAG AND META DESCRIPTIONS

The title tag and meta descriptions for each of your web pages are two of the most important factors for the Click-Through Rate of your web pages. Just because you have a website doesn't mean people will visit it, and just because you rank your website well doesn't mean anyone will click on the website you were able to rank. Optimizing your title tag and meta description is the exact strategy you need to get customers who find your site to click through to it.

When optimizing your title tag and meta description, you must first do some competitive research.

- What keywords are they using?
- How many of a certain keyword are they using?
- What phrases or questions do they use?

One of the running themes of this book is that you are not competing with Google, and this is a perfect example. To improve your rank, use the keyword you are ranking for more times in your title tag and meta description than your competitors are.

You also want to put yourself in your customers' shoes. What are they searching for, and how can your title tag and meta description provide the right information they need that would make them interested in learning more? Are you solving their problem and providing what they need?

Title tags should be about 60 characters in length, and the meta description should be about 155-160 characters.

When optimizing to please your customer and adding keywords, make sure they relate to the page you are driving them to. If your title tag and meta description are irrelevant to the page you are allowing the customer to click to, you will increase your bounce rate and potentially lose rankings.

Tips for optimizing your title tag and meta description

- Avoid duplicate titles and descriptions
- Keep the length proper for display
- Include relevant keywords
- Don't keyword stuff
- Put the most important words first
- Include your brand name in title tags
- Include action verbs like "shop now" or "learn our secrets"
- Use value propositions like "free online quote"
- Capitalize important words
- Add review schema to get 5 stars in your description

CHAPTER 12 REVIEW

1. What is the current CTR for each of your target pages?

2. Based on the best practices in this chapter, what will you do to each page to improve your CTR?

CHAPTER 13

OPTIMIZING ECOMMERCE PRODUCT PAGES

Author: Allison Lee - Zentail

Navigating SEO can get tricky as you're building out your eCommerce site. In this bonus chapter, Allison Lee from Zentail, an eCommerce automation platform, shares practical tips for getting your product pages up to snuff and outranking competitors.

When creating your main site, keep in mind that search engines are looking to showcase sites that are trustworthy and easy to navigate. The general rule of thumb is that everything should be accessible within three clicks. In other words, after landing on your homepage, your buyers should be able to find any product in three or less clicks.

To that end, you need to make sure that your site architecture is clear and simple. Offer just enough top-level categories and filters to guide your buyers in the right direction—and make sure there's a clear, consistent hierarchy to your pages.

From there, your product pages deserve a fair amount of attention. Not only are they instrumental in driving sales, but they offer a way to rank on less competitive terms than your homepage. Here are several things you'll want to keep an eye on as you work through your product pages.

KEYWORDS

Tedious as it may sound, you should be performing keyword research on *each* page. If you have a large website, you can begin by prioritizing pages that drive the most conversions or earn the most visitors—then approach the rest of your site in phases.

Follow the steps in Chapter 9 when performing keyword research and remember to evaluate search intent. For example, if you're looking to optimize a page around a bag of dog treats you're selling but see that nine out of 10 first-page results for "dog treats" are blogs, not product pages, look for more relevant variations that attract visitors with an intent to purchase.

Just like with blog posts, you'll want to include your primary keyword (and some related words) in your on-page copy and in your meta titles and descriptions. While it's best to customize meta titles and descriptions for every page, you can take a templated approach to some pages to make this part a little easier. Here's an example of a meta title and description template that could work.

{Product Name} | Organic Dog Treats | MyBrand

Buy {Product Name} dog treats made from natural, healthy ingredients. Enjoy free shipping on any orders over $35.

Reserve this approach for certain categories or subcategories where it makes sense. In general, there's no substitute for original copy, especially when it comes to your most important product pages.

Content Depth and Uniqueness

When you're in a rush or in a creative rut, it may be tempting to slap up an image, title, and a few bullet points on your product page, then hit publish. But by resorting to "thin" content, you significantly lower your chances of ranking on search engines.

Google and other engines favor information-rich pages. Some of the highest-ranking product pages feature 1,000+ words of high-quality content. Search engines use these details to understand what your page is about and evaluate its trustworthiness. In the same vein, you'll want to make sure your product descriptions are unique. Avoid copying and pasting descriptions from manufacturers' sites or using the same copy as you do on other pages of your site or another eCommerce platform like Amazon.

This will help you stand out from the competition and avoid duplicate content, which can confuse search engines as they try to index your page. If the search engine finds hundreds of pages that look like near duplicates on your site, it will only pick one of those versions to show (if any). Or, if you have two identical product pages —one on your site and the other on Amazon—the Amazon version will almost always beat your original listing since Amazon already has a high domain authority.

Optimized Images

Images have a special place in eCommerce for obvious (and over-stated) reasons. From an SEO standpoint, they're equally important because they improve your site's user experience and visibility. For instance, you can make sure that your products appear in relevant image searches with optimized images.

To ensure that your images are crawlable, take a look at your image titles and avoid uploading those titled "IMG1001.png." Instead, use a more descriptive title like "blue-waterproof-jacket.png" to help search engines index your content properly.

Alt text (aka, "alt attributes" or "alt tags") is another important feature. Besides providing extra context for search engine crawlers, alt text helps visually impaired users access your site. Screen readers will read the alt text that you provide to describe the image at hand.

The best format for alt text is descriptive but not too wordy. So, for an image of a blue waterproof jacket, you might use the alt text "female student wearing blue waterproof jacket." This lets the reader know that the jacket is designed for young women without requiring too much time to read or stuffing a bunch of keywords unnaturally.

Beyond this, you'll want to make sure that the file sizes for your images are as small as possible; large image files are notorious for killing site load speed. As part of your uploading process, compress your product images using free tools like TinyPNG or Compressor.io. Create separate, smaller images for any thumbnails and consider letting a bit of the quality slide here if it means faster loading times.

VARIATIONS

Product variations can add an extra layer of confusion when it comes to SEO. You might be wondering, "How do I avoid duplicate content (or keyword cannibalization) when I've got a dozen pages related to the same product?"

Ideally, you'd only have one main URL for your variations. You can do this by combining your variations onto a single page and utilizing things like drop-down menus for buyers to easily browse their options. This makes sure that even as the content on the screen changes, the URL remains the same.

If you prefer to have separate pages for your variations (you want to be able to link to individual pages to fill up blank space on your site when you're just getting started), then use rel="canonical" tags in the <head></head> section of your secondary pages so that they point to one authoritative URL.

If you're concerned about losing keyword traffic associated with individual variations, consider how splitting information across multiple pages or having duplicate content can dilute your over SEO power. Chances are that you can still rank for those variant-specific keywords if you have one high-performing product page that mentions those details.

CROSS-CHANNEL PROMOTION

"Just because you built it, doesn't mean they'll come." This saying is especially true in SEO, where quality content alone won't cut it. You *need* to take extra steps to ensure that people find and regularly engage with your content, signaling to search engines that your content truly satisfies the needs of your visitors.

Test various tools at your disposal: emails, social media, public relations, ads, remarketing, etc. Many Zentail users take advantage of Surfaces across Google, first and foremost, because it's free. As long as you've got your site connected to Google Merchant Center with a properly formatted product feed, you can opt into Surfaces and display your products across Google Images, the Google Shopping tab, Google Lens, and more. (Alternatively, if your site already has correctly structured data markup, you'll automatically be shown on most Google Surfaces.)

Once you're set up in the Merchant Center, it's easy to get started with Shopping Ads as well. This is Google's pay-per-click ad program which showcases your products at the top of search results.

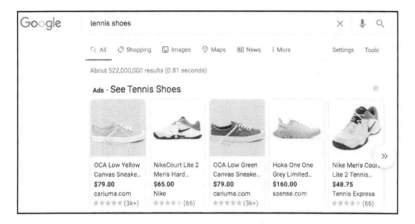

Ads will also appear prominently across the Shopping tab, Google Images, and other affiliate sites like YouTube.

It's a good idea to leverage tools like this to get your name out there and accelerate your chances of ranking high on SERPs.

CHAPTER 14

Performing a Technical Audit

Author: Roger Bryan - Growth Foundry

You should review your site's audit report every month and determine what on-site technical optimization is required for the month. Ensuring websites are free from critical site audit errors will help prevent the website from being penalized by Google. The more errors a website has, the harder it will be to rank that website.

Site Audits

The first step in the on-site technical optimization process is to run a full site audit. We recommend using two tools at the same time. The first tool is SEMRush site auditor, and the second is the site audit tool in Agency Analytics. Both tools can point out any critical issues the site is facing from a technical perspective.

Here is an example of what a site audit looks like

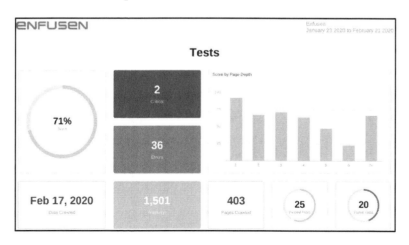

Once the site audit is completed, tackle the critical errors first because those will directly penalize the website from an overall SEO perspective. Examples of some of the common critical errors include:

- 505 Server Errors
- 404 Errors
- Broken External Links
- Broken Internal Links
- Duplicate Content

It is important that every month you focus on 1-2 errors that are apparent on the site and fix them. It normally takes around 30 days for the error to disappear from the audit, which is why we recommend running one every 30 days.

SITE SPEED

Site Audits are only one part of the overall technical optimization of a site. You should always have your eye on the website's speed. We have included a detailed section on this at the end of the book under "Additional Resources," but it is extremely important to understand the speed of the site and mitigate any loading issues. We have worked with clients who have seen a complete loss of mobile rankings because their site speed was above average. To test the speed of a website, we recommend using the tool available at GTMetrix.com.

Some common ways to solve site speed errors:

- Compress all images on your site
- Disable plugins that take a long time to load
- Remove any unnecessary tracking codes from your site

We have had success hiring speed optimization professionals who can completely turn a website's speed and load time into above average numbers for a couple hundred dollars.

BACKLINK AUDITS

Another important technical site optimization is backlink audits. If your client has a website that has been around for a long time, they most likely have hundreds or thousands of backlinks coming to their site. There is a good possibility that 20% of those links are toxic or spammy, which can hurt a website's overall optimization score for SEO. I recommend that you review your client's site twice a year by running a backlink audit and disavowing any toxic links to Google. The benefit of cleaning up the backlinks from a website not only includes the positive SEO impact but also gives you a clean list of links that you can use for tiered link building, which can provide major SEO value.

CHAPTER 14 REVIEW

1. What tool will you use for technical site audits?

2. After running your site audit, what the three major issues will you address first?

CHAPTER 15

OPTIMIZE FOR MOBILE

Author: Roger Bryan - Growth Foundry

SITE LOAD SPEED

The core aspect of optimizing a site for mobile is to increase its load speed. The first thing to understand is that there is no single metric or measurement for 'speed.' There's no simple number that you can use to measure how quickly your pages load.

Think about what happens when you load a website. There are many stages and different parts that can be measured. If the network connection is slow, but the images load quickly, how 'fast' is the site? What about the other way around?

For example, a page that takes longer to 'finish loading' may provide a functional 'lightweight' version while the full page is still downloading in the background. Is that 'faster' or 'slower' than a website that loads faster, but which I can't use until it's finished loading?

The answer is, "it depends," and there are many different ways in which we can think about or measure 'site speed.'

Site speed is one of the factors that determine whether you get a good ranking in Google. Site speed is a ranking factor, and its importance keeps growing. A slow website will result in a slower crawling rate, so Google indexes pages on your site at a slower rate. New posts will take longer to show up in the search results. Therefore, making your website faster can lead to getting organic traffic for new posts faster and better rankings. Research shows that people don't buy as much or read as much on slower sites.

THE BEST SITE SPEED TOOLS

When analyzing a website's SEO, we always check the site speed. Site speed varies when checking it from different locations, which is one reason why speed tools do not always provide the same results. So, we use all of these tools when testing a site (and do not rely on only one):

1. Google Mobile Tester

   https://search.Google.com/test/mobile-friendly

2. Pingdom Website Speed Test Tools

   http://Tools.Pingdom.com/fpt/Edit

3. GTMetrix

   https://GTMetrix.com/Edit

4. WebPageTest

   www.WebPageTest.org/Edit

5. Google Lighthouse

   https://Developers.Google.com/web/tools/lighthouse/edit

6. Google PageSpeed Insights

   Splits mobile and desktop and has recently been updated to use more real-world data to give more usable results. Also, its suggestions to fix speed issues have been improved.

7. Pingdom's Website Speed Test Tools

Allows for multiple locations and GTmetrix combines several checks nicely.

8.   WebPageTest

Has a few main checks it grades in an easy to understand manner.

9.   Yoast.com

Built into Chrome and was originally meant to assess Progressive Web Apps. However, it gives great insights into the page speed and user experience of your mobile site based on real-world tests.

We recommend you use all of these tools to check your site speed. Combined, they give a complete overview of the speed of your site.

If you want to test your site speed, you can enter the URL of your website in the tools listed above. They review the speed of your site and provide a list of options to improve it. Most of the tools have reasonably good, though slightly techy, explanations on the various aspects that you can improve upon. Unfortunately, some of these are a bit hard to interpret.

WordPress plugins to speed up your site

Installing a caching plugin could really speed up your site if your hosting doesn't already provide for caching.

WP Super Cache

https://nl.wordpress.org/plugins/wp-super-cache/Edit

AMP plugin

AMP, short for Accelerated Mobile Pages, is another effort by Google to increase the speed of the web.

Yoast News SEO Plugin

Yoast.com/setting-up-wordpress-for-amp-accelerated-mobile-pages/edit

Besides installing a caching plugin, you can do several other things to speed up your site. Choosing a different hosting party, using a CDN, and/or minifying your images could do wonders for your site speed. We'll come back to you regularly with site speed solutions and talk you through the most important ones.

There's no single metric.

Understanding the Loading Process

From the moment you click on a link (or hit 'enter' in your URL bar), a process begins to load the page you requested.

That process contains many steps, but they can be grouped into broad stages which looks something like this:

The "one-second timeline" from Google's site speed documentation

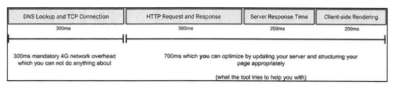

DNS Lookup and TCP Connection	HTTP Request and Response	Server Response Time	Client-side Rendering
300ms	300ms	200ms	200ms

300ms mandatory 4G network overhead which you can not do anything about

700ms which you can optimize by updating your server and structuring your page appropriately

(what the tool tries to help you with)

While Google's documentation might be a bit ambitious about the timings of these stages, the model is helpful. Essentially, the process can be described as three stages of loading.

1. NETWORK STUFF

First, the physical hardware of your device needs to connect to the internet. Usually, that involves moving data through transatlantic fiber cables, which means that you're limited by the speed of light and how quickly your device can process information.

It's hard to measure or impact this part of the process!

2. SERVER STUFF

Here, your device asks your server for a page, and the server prepares and returns the response.

This section can get a bit technical because it's focused on the performance of server hardware, databases, and scripts. You may need to ask your hosting provider or tech team for help.

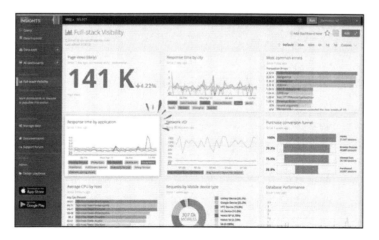

NEWRELIC

We can measure the performance of the server with tools like NewRelic or DataDog, which monitors how your site behaves and responds from the 'inside'.

They can provide charts and metrics around things like slow database queries and slow scripts. Armed with this information, you can better understand if your hosting is up to scratch and determine if you need to make code changes to your theme/plugins/scripts.

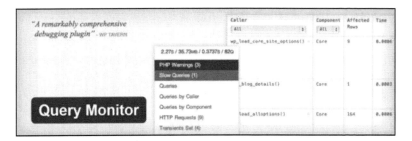

THE QUERY MONITOR PLUGIN FOR WORDPRESS

WordPress has some great plugins for doing this kind of analysis, too. I'm a big fan of Query Monitor, which provides some great insight into the bits of WordPress that might be slowing you down (themes, plugins, or environments.

3. BROWSER STUFF

This stage is where the page needs to be constructed, laid out, colored in, and displayed. The way in which images load, how JavaScript and CSS are processed, and every individual HTML tag on your page affects how quickly things load.

We can monitor some of this from the 'outside-in' with tools that scan the website and measure how it loads. We recommend using multiple tools, as they measure things differently and are useful for various assessments.

Use an 'outside-in' tool, like WebPageTest to generate a waterfall diagram of how the website loads.

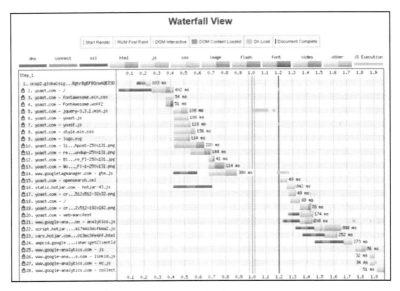

WebPageTest results for yoast.com

These kinds of tools are great for spotting things like images which need to be optimized, where your CSS or JavaScript is slow, or where you're waiting for assets to load from other domains.

WRAPPING THIS INTO A PROCESS

Identify bottlenecks with servers and the back end. Look for slow connection times, slow SSL handshakes, and slow DNS lookups.

Use a plugin like https://en-gb.WordPress.org/plugins/query-monitor/ or a service like https://NewRelic.com/ to diagnose what's holding things up. Make server, hardware, software and script changes.

Identify bottlenecks with the front end. Look for slow loading and processing times on images, scripts and stylesheets. Use a tool like https://developers.Google.com/speed/pagespeed/insights/ or https://Chrome.Google.com/webstore/detail/lighthouse/blipmdconl kpinefehnmjammfjpmpbjk?hl=en for suggestions on how to streamline how the page loads.

To measure your key metrics, like time until first meaningful paint and time until interactive, use
https://chrome.google.com/webstore/detail/lighthouse/blip-mdconlkpinefehnmjammfjpmpbjk?hl=en

CHAPTER 15 REVIEW

1. Does your site pass the Google Mobile Optimization Test?

2. What are three issues you found while using the other available tools that you would like to improve on your mobile site?

LOCAL SCHEMA MARKUP

Author: Roger Bryan - Growth Foundry

Site Schema is a new optimization strategy that is becoming more critical to ranking your page. Schema tells the search engines what your data means, not just what it says. In this chapter, I will guide you through implementing site schema markup, managing multi-location schema, and outline the best strategies for optimizing local landing pages.

SITE SCHEMA MARKUP GUIDE

1. **Go to www.google.com/webmasters/markup-helper/u/0/**

2. **Determine the kind of data you will be marking up**

3. **Paste your specific URL at the bottom and click "start tagging"**

   You will be taken to a screen that shows your website on the left and the data markup tool on the right. This is where you will start tagging your content.

4. **Tag your content**

   Depending on the type of data markup category you chose, you will be able to tag specific pieces of content. To tag content, you want to highlight the specific word and tag it accordingly.

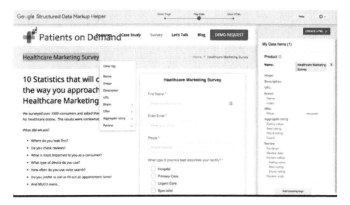

   In the example above, "Healthcare Marketing Survey" is highlighted and tagged as the "name" of the product.

   The list to the right titled "My Data Items" shows the list of all the items you can tag on your web page. Make sure to tag as many data items as possible. Schema.org's instructions clearly state, "the more content you mark up, the better."

   http://schema.org/docs/gs.html#microdata_itemscope_itemtype

   Pro Tip: If your web page is missing specific data items that are able to be tagged, we highly recommend adding them to your page so that you receive the maximum effect from your site schema. If you are missing items, add them and then continue with the markup process as you need to do the markup one time for maximum effectiveness.

5. Click "Create HTML"

Once you are done with your markup, click "Create HTML"

6. Retrieve your HTML code

You will see the HTML of your page with the relevant micro data inserted in the spots that you selected (the micro data is highlighted in yellow)

7. Add the code to your web page

The easiest method to add the markup is to download the automatically generated HTML file, copy/paste it into the back end of your web page.

The more tedious method is going through the code generated and copy/paste each yellow highlighted section individually.

When you click "Finish," you will be presented with a series of "Next Steps."

8. Test your page using the Structured Data Testing Tool search.google.com/structured-data/testing-tool/u/0/

Once the code is added to your site, use the Structured Data Testing Tool which to see what your page will look like in Google search results. If there is an error, you can edit the HTML directly in the testing tool to update the schema and preview results again.

CHAPTER 16 REVIEW

1. Did you install your local schema markup on each of your location pages (or your main location page if you only have one)?

2. Did you test your schema markup using https://search.Google.com/structured-data/testing-tool/u/0/?

CHAPTER 17

Link Building

Author: Roger Bryan - Growth Foundry

According to Google, "Webmasters can improve the rank of their sites by increasing the number of high-quality sites that link to their pages." Link building is a long-standing strategy that many marketing experts have in their toolbox. But you don't need to be a marketing expert to create a backlink strategy that will bring long-term benefit and rank increase to your website. This chapter will discuss the top six types of links and go through how you can use them, what not to do, how well the link works, and where to find the links. Once you finish reading this chapter, you will be able to create a link building strategy that works for your website and will increase your rank.

Six Link Building Strategies to Boost Your SEO Efforts and Rank Your Website

1. HIGH VALUE PRESS RELEASE (PR INDIVIDUAL LIKE RICHARD LORENZEN)

A high-value press release has a high price tag, but this strategy has a worthy outcome. A high-quality press release can shed positive light on your business, provide backlinks, are completely natural, and will prevent your site from getting penalized. When you publish a press release with a high-value firm, you will also receive even higher authority backlinks because of their premium distribution channels, like USA Today, Forbes, Inc, etc.

How to use PRs: Use these for the most important page you are trying to rank on your site and your most important keywords. This type of press release is not cheap because of the value it holds. When creating the press release, it is critical you create a title that will catch the reader's attention and drive more clicks to your site.

What not to do: Don't use this type of press release without ensuring the content is quality. Also, make sure you use the proper links within your press release, or most of the value will be lost. When working with clients, we always look for major announcements that we could create a press release about and then tie in an important page and keyword that will gain the value.

Where can you get this link: There are several high-value press release firms that you can contact, such as FifthAvenueBrands.com.

How well does this link work: This is one of the best links money can buy. You will receive hundreds of high-quality authentic links. When using this strategy, think quality over quantity – use sparingly for your important pages only.

2. EDITORIAL LINKS

So far, we have covered higher price items and heavy lift strategies, but editorial content can be an easy way to drive links to your site without paying for an expensive service or spending time creating a website. An editorial mention occurs when another website links back to or mentions your site in a piece of content. Some examples of editorial links are citing someone from your company, linking to your website as a resource for information, citing your website as the creator of a graphic, image, or infographic, or an interview with someone from your website.

How to Use Editorial Links: To get editorial mentions, start creating content on your site that could be considered a "go-to source of information." Having high-quality blog posts that pertain to a specific industry could lead other platforms to share your expertise or link back to it to drive customers to the source of truth. You also want to create content that can easily be shared, such as informative graphics, guides, or checklists that people can use secondhand and give your site credit for the information.

What not to do: Spend your time creating high-quality content that is not sought after in your industry. Keep up on current trends and complete keyword research to understand what the industry is looking for, so your work is of value.

Where can you get this link: You can get editorial links by creating high-quality content on your site that is shared throughout your industry.

How well does this link work: The value of these links is completely dependent on the site that is linking back to yours. If you get a link from your local newspaper compared to Forbes.com, the value will change, but this should be viewed as an ongoing marketing effort that will provide long-term benefit.

3. GUEST POST LINKS

Guest post links are generated when you submit a guest post to another website and include a link back to your website. These links help to build trust, and this strategy should be added to your website's marketing toolbox. In an article written by ahrefs, they discuss how using guest post blogging can help you build links at scale.

How to use them and what not to do: Do not expect an increase in your website's SEO after one guest post. Make sure the guest posts you create are related to the website and industry you are trying to drive value towards.

Where can you get this link: Find guest websites that will allow you to be a regular guest blogger and start creating content to post on guest sites that will help you build trust within your industry and be newsworthy to the guest site.

How well does this link work: If you use this link building tactic consistently over time, this can become a very powerful source of authority for your website and allow your site to become an "expert" in the industry for which you are guest blogging.

4. TIERED LINKS

Tiered links is the process of building tiers of links to a target site. For the first tier, create high-quality content links such as the high-quality press release. Next, drive a hundred links to that first tier of high-quality links to increase the value called second tier links. To avoid being penalized, make sure the second tier of links to your high-quality links are not spammy (these could be guest blog posts, or you can also reach out to other companies and ask them to link to your site). Next, create your third tier which you can build by hiring someone on Fiverr that has great feedback and good history.

How to Use Tiered Links: Find someone reliable on Fiverr or Upwork who has good feedback and consistently delivers.

What not to do: Do not pay $5 for hundreds of spammy links that could penalize your site and flag it to Google.

Where can you get this link: To create the first tier, use the press release strategy, which will get you the foundation of the high-quality links. To get the other two tiers, search Fiverr and Upwork and find someone with high reviews and good quality tiered links.

How well does this link work: Tiered links work well but should be used in moderation. You cannot use this method multiple times for the same site in a month or you will get flagged. Just like the press release is only used for your most important pages and key-words, this should be used as an add-on when you use the press release strategy to enhance the value.

5. BUFFER LINKS

A buffer link is created when you build out a website dedicated to a specific topic and post high-quality content on a weekly basis that links back to multiple different sites with the same topic, sometimes your site. Using buffer links is a risky technique, and we recommend doing extensive research before implementing on your site.

How to use Buffer Links: To create buffer links, create a website that provides expertise on a specific topic. Some sites you can use include Jimbdo, Webnode, and Weebly. The site should be fully built out with proper information and high-quality content (900+ words) posted on a bi-weekly basis. When you post this content, you can link back to your site creating a stream of backlinks related to the exact keyword you are looking to improve rank on.

What not to do: Do NOT create a 2-page site and add short, low-quality blog posts every once and a while.

Where can you get this link: If you don't have time to create high-quality sites to generate links, you can buy links. Several services allow you to purchase links on their buffer sites. Be wary of these services and make sure you only trust those with a good track record and experience.

How well does this link work: This link is one of the more powerful links, but it does take a lot of time and energy to create multiple sites and have consistent bi-weekly content pieces that will bring the value your site needs. If your business has the resources, this strategy would be well worth your time. Be mindful that the buffer link technique is riskier than others and can sometimes be considered a black hat technique. If you are using this strategy, it is important to know all the details and implement it according to webmaster rules to avoid penalties of your site.

6. AUTHORITY LINKS

Authority links are links from other sites that have established substantial trust and authority with search engines due to the site's age, quality, size, and activity level. Examples of authority sites include government sites, educational organizations, large institutions, or leading industry sites. The higher the authority on the site, the more rank power it will bring to that link.

How to use Authority Links: Use high authority links for the pages you need help ranking that are currently on the second page but need to be put on the first page

What not to do: Don't expect to pay $200 for 100 high-authority links. They are powerful because they are hard to get.

Where can you get this link: One way to get this link is to create high-quality content that would be of interest to a high authority site. You can offer this content and put a link to your site within the content. You can also order a high authority press release which can get your press release distributed to a variety of high authority sites. The last tactic, although it does not always work, is simply asking or emailing high authority sites to link to your site. According to Neil Patel, there are 11 ways you can get authority links. Read his article at https://neilpatel.com/blog/11-ways-to-get-authority-links-for-your-new-blog/.

How well does this link work: High authority links will stick with your site for a very long time and bring a lot of value. They are not easily accessible or cheap, but when built into a long-term strategy, can eventually give your site more authority.

For SEO, there are a variety of different links that can bring value to your website. We recommend adding link building to your short-term and long-term strategy to receive maximum benefits. If you want to determine how many backlinks you have pointing to your site, we try using this free backlink checker tool https://www.seoreviewtools.com/valuable-backlinks-checker/

574	47%	152	194
External backlinks Pointing to: page	Follow links (Percentage)	Referring Domains Pointing to: page	Referring IP's Pointing to: page

CHAPTER 17 REVIEW

1. What will be your initial link building strategy?
2. How will you go about getting the needed links?

CHAPTER 18

4 Ways PR Can Help Your SEO Campaign

Author Richard Lorenzen – Fifth Avenue Brands

PR and SEO go hand-in-hand, and an effective public relations strategy can play a significant role in the success of your search engine optimization efforts. The entire digital ecosystem is constantly evolving, and today, more than ever, PR has a direct impact on SEO.

High-quality content and outreach are mandatory for a successful SEO campaign, which is exactly what PR is built around. PR has its own strategy and direct benefits, but when you understand how it also impacts your business's success in Google's organic search results, it helps you realize just how important – and mandatory – it is.

Here are four examples of how PR can help your SEO campaign, directly contributing to more organic exposure and website traffic

1. Earn High Quality Backlinks.

Backlinks have always been, and will continue to be, the number one 'signal' that Google's algorithm uses to determine where your website shows up in the organic search results for keywords and search phrases relevant to the content on your pages.

There are hundreds factors, but links are still the biggest contributor, although the types of links that Google loves has most certainly evolved over the years, and this is where PR comes into play.

It's no longer about quantity when it comes to links – it's all about quality. The most desired links are from high-quality websites and publications, and these are not links that you can simply buy; they must be earned, and a well-executed PR strategy can help you secure the most desirable links within your industry.

2. Dominate the SERPs for Your Brand Name and Keywords.

PR campaigns are designed to get publications talking about you and your business. When done successfully, this results in several placements and mentions on high-authority outlets. The content on these authority-leading websites typically ranks high in the organic search results, which helps fill the top with content related to you and your business.

When someone searches for your or your business and they see your brand name on top outlets, it paints a very positive picture and helps instill consumer confidence almost immediately.

Filling up the top of the search results page with content that you essentially control is also a good strategy for brand protection in the event that an upset customer or a competitor writes something negative online.

3. Leverage High Authority Websites to Rank for Keywords Your Website Won't Rank for.

Ranking your website for specific keywords is sometimes very difficult, because major players like Amazon, Apple, or Walmart dominate the top spots. While you may not be able to reach the top on your own website, you can often leverage the authority of PR targets to rank on top and then use that placement to drive traffic back to your website.

When the PR effort is executed with SEO in mind, the article titles and content can be designed to target specific keywords and search queries that you want your brand to pull traffic from.

4. Trigger More Brand Search Queries — Which is Beneficial For Google's Algorithm

PR is designed to create buzz for your brand, and when done correctly, results in more people searching for more information. When you land a placement via PR, your brand is put in front of a new audience. If the piece is done well, readers become interested in learning more and search for more information.

These brand search queries are highly beneficial, as Google sees this as a sign of brand popularity and begins to place more weight on your website when determining where your content will show in the results. If two websites have similar authority and similar content, Google will display the one with more brand search queries in the higher position, as it assumes that's what its users wants to see.

REVIEWS, REVIEWS, REVIEWS

According to The Hosting Tribunal, "Reviews are the most crucial part of the purchase decision for 90% of US." And reviews are not just important to the customers' purchase decision but also to search engines. The more positive reviews you have for a business, the more credible your business becomes online. One of the most important places for reviews is your Google My Business (GMB) listing. Adding reviews to your GMB profile is critical in remaining competitive among other businesses and will help you increase the rank of your online presence. It will also make sure that when customers find you online, they are more inclined to click through to your site because they see a positive number of reviews, making them feel secure about their purchasing decision.

One of the best ways to get reviews is by adding a review loop into your marketing strategy. One method we used for a client to gain back their maps listings was to implement a review loop that allowed them to enter back into the map 3 pack. You first need to create a page on the website with the URL structure *https://www.Website-Name/Reviews.*

On the page, you should only have two buttons and header text. The header text should say, "How did we do?" Below the header, there should be two buttons – one green button that says "Great!" and one red button that says, "Not so Good." Based on the customer's decision, they will be sent to two different pages. We want to make sure that we don't allow customers with a negative experience to leave a review but instead contact the team to mitigate the situation.

If the customer chooses the green "Great!" button, they are directed to leave a review directly on the Google My Business listing.

For some clients, we have added multiple review locations (Facebook, Yelp, GMB), so depending on the account the customer has, they can leave a review.

If the customer chooses the red "Not so Good" button, they are directed to another page with a form that allows them to describe the bad experience and check a box that permits a member of the team to contact them to understand how they can make this customer feel better about the situation.

Once you have these pages set up, we recommend testing the process on a list of customers from the previous month. Make sure to keep a close eye on the email's open, click, and bounce rates.

If creating a review loop doesn't work for your client's business, there are other options, including working with a reputation management company that is specific to your client's niche industry. If your client has a physical location, you can set up an iPad to accept customer reviews directly after an appointment or meeting to ensure a timely review process.

CHAPTER 16 REVIEW

1. How many reviews do you need to overtake the competition in your local market?

2. What strategy will you use to get the needed reviews?

Bounce Rate Optimization

Author: Roger Bryan - Growth Foundry

Why does bounce rate matter?

When a user (e.g., customer, prospect, or reader) visits your site on any page (known as an entrance page) and leaves without visiting other pages on the same domain, that's a bounce. Your bounce rate is the percentage of all users who enter and exit on the same page, without any clicks to other pages on your site.

If you have a high bounce rate, you're not attracting the right site visitor or the visitors coming don't have a good user experience.

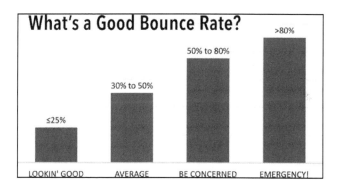

1. Improve Content Readability

A customer has a good experience when the content is well organized and easy to read (7th grade level). A great way to improve readability is to use subheadings (H2, H3, H4, etc.) when formatting your page. This allows the reader to see the breakdown of content easily on your page.

Bullet points are an excellent way to showcase the most important parts of your page. Once your content is written, pick out the key benefits you want your audience to take away and make a bullet point list.

2. USE PLENTY OF CHARTS, IMAGES, SCREENSHOTS, AND QUOTES WHERE APPROPRIATE.

One way to gain the reader's attention is to use visual aids within the content of your page. Many readers remember the visual aspects more than the written content. Images, charts, or screenshots can help explain complex material or provide more detail to the content already written.

3. BOLD KEYWORDS WHEN NECESSARY

Bolding keywords can help showcase the primary focus and topic of your page but don't overdo it. Only bold your keyword 2-3 times in the entire body of the page; it's not necessary to bold every instance of the keyword. Use it sparingly but effectively.

4. USE BULLET POINTS TO EXPLAIN BENEFITS OR POINTS WORTH NOTING TO BREAK UP PARAGRAPHS OF TEXT

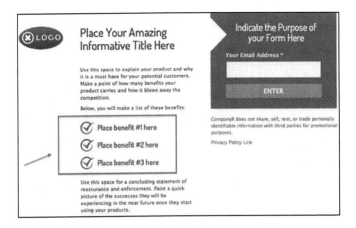

5. USE STORYTELLING TO CAPTIVATE YOUR AUDIENCE

According to Adam Toren, people are wired to remember powerful stories, and adding them to your content can help bring your brand to life. Not only does storytelling help your page, but it also appeals to the user's emotions. A great story alone can create a great page of content that will help improve your bounce rate and time on site.

6. ASK QUESTIONS IN YOUR CONTENT

By asking multiple questions in your content, you are giving readers an invitation to participate instead of only reading your content.

7. END YOUR CONTENT WITH A SUBHEADING ENTITLED "CONCLUSION"

This tells the reader to quickly read the last few words and take action. It is important that once a customer finishes the content on your page, they have an actionable step that will drive them deeper into your funnel to becoming a customer. The biggest mistake you can make is giving a customer a great page without an action for them to take.

8. ADD VIDEOS TO YOUR CONTENT

Another great way to keep users from exiting your page is to give them something to do, and what is better than watching a video? A video can be an extremely powerful piece of content to enhance your page and even your rankings. If you are adding a video, make sure it is:

- Relevant to the primary keyword of the page
- Structured properly to include video schema
- 30 seconds – 3 minutes long
- Embedded straight on your page and not just a clickable link

Check out our blog post on the exact steps you need to take to get your videos to rank on Google.

9. Use bright colors that grab the user's attention

Colors play a large part in the user experience of your page. When creating your landing page, use bright colors that will grab the user's attention and make them want to stay on the page. With properly structured content, bright colors, and visual aids, a user will be more inclined to spend time exploring your website instead of bouncing.

10. Increase Page Load Time

Page load time plays a large role in the bounce rate of your page. According to Kissmetrics, 47% of consumers expect a page to load in two seconds or less. It is vital that your page loads quickly on all devices because all it takes is a few seconds for a customer to click out and find a new page.

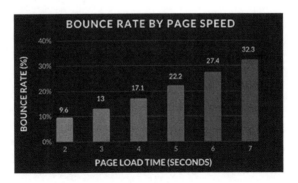

11. SET EXTERNAL LINKS TO OPEN IN A NEW WINDOW

One of the biggest mistakes that marketers make is having external links open in the same window. Sometimes a reader just wants to view more information but not lose the current page. By allowing external links to open in new windows, you ensure the customer doesn't leave the page until they are ready to exit.

12. CREATE A GOOD CALL-TO-ACTION (CTA)

A good call to action can make all the difference when trying to convert your page views into customers. But creating the best CTA isn't just a catchy sentence. Below are a few tips you want to use when crafting the perfect call to action:

- Have multiple CTAs that allow the customer to navigate to different areas on your site.
- Position the first CTA above the fold of the page so the reader is able to take action within three seconds.
- Make sure the CTA is relevant to the users reading your content.
- Your CTA should compel users to NEED to see what is on the other side of the button.
- Use a color opposite of the color palette of your page so it stands out to the reader.

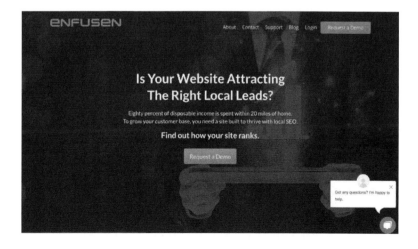

Get our experts to do all the work - https://growthfoundry.com/rank-me

13. ADD HELPFUL INTERNAL LINKS TO YOUR CONTENT

Adding internal links to your content can help navigate the reader to other parts of your website that may meet their needs more than the current page they are on. Within your page, make sure you are linking to other service lines, products, or further information that could drive the reader closer to becoming a customer.

14. USE RELEVANT ANCHOR TEXT

Using proper anchor text makes a significant difference in your content. Anchor text can provide relevant contextual information about the content of the link's destination to search engines and users.

15. TEST YOUR CONTENT

Once your page is completed, test it using read-able.com. This website will tell you how readable your site is and what needs to be fixed to have a page easy enough for a user to digest.

CHAPTER 19 REVIEW

1. What is the bounce rate of each of your target pages?

2. What will you do to each page to improve their bounce rate?

CHAPTER 20

INTERNAL LINKING

Author: Roger Bryan - Growth Foundry

An internal link is a link that points to another page on the same website. The descriptive keywords in the anchor text tell the reader the topic of the page to which they are being linked.

In the image below, you will see we created an internal link that can take the customer to two of our blog posts to learn more about marketing strategies. We did this because the customer was already reading a blog post about different marketing strategies, so linking to others along the same topic can take the customer deeper into our website.

WHY IS INTERNAL LINKING IMPORTANT?

There are four core reasons why internal linking is important.

1. Allows users to navigate your website easily and find more relevant content related to what they are looking for.

2. Establish an information hierarchy for your website.

3. Help spread link equity (ranking power) around your website.

4. Help search engines assess the relationship of your site's internal pages

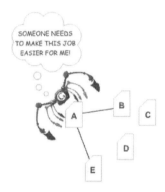

Internal linking strengthens the overall SEO value of a website by providing clear paths for spiders, prolonged sessions for users, and a tight-knit network of pages and posts. When your website has strong internal linking, the Google crawler can more easily find new content that you post.

HOW TO IMPLEMENT INTERNAL LINKING FOR YOUR WEBSITE

1. CREATE A CONTENT STARTING POINT

To get started with link building, make sure you have multiple content pages on your site, such as landing pages, case study pages, service pages, or blog posts. Even if you just start with 1-2 pages or posts, you need to make sure you have something to link to with a congruent topic.

Pro Tip: When determining what content to create, use Google Search Console or other marketing tools that can tell you what your customers are searching for. Once you have a few good topics, write a blog post for each one that can educate your customer.

2. BE CONSISTENT IN ADDING CONTENT

Make sure content creation is a priority within your business. Consistently creating links allows you to always be present to Google.

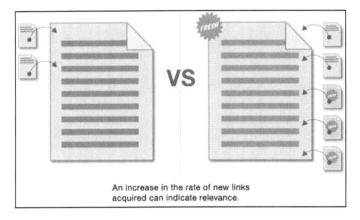

An increase in the rate of new links acquired can indicate relevance.

Adding new content is even more important since Google updated their algorithm in 2017 to include "website freshness" as a factor in ranking websites. According to *Search Engine Journal*, "If your content hasn't been refreshed or updated in some time, it will be surpassed for more engaging, fresh, and new competing content." Along with bringing fresh content to your site, Google also looks at the frequency of content related to a topic.

For all of these reasons, being consistent when adding content to your site can be one of the most important factors of link building.

3. UPDATE OLD CONTENT WITH INTERNAL LINKS

According to Neil Patel, "Every time you write an article, link to four or more old articles."

We recommend that you always use at least two internal links when creating content pieces like blog posts.

4. LEVERAGE YOUR BLOG POSTS

Start the linking process with your blog posts. The best internal links are from blog post to blog post. Because you are providing educational content and answers to customer questions with your blog posts, it poses you as an expert for that topic and is a great place to use internal linking.

Helpful Hints: Do not link to your About Us, Contact Us, or Homepage because these don't provide as much link equity and will not provide value to your customer. Focus on landing pages, blog posts, case study pages, or other pages that provide extensive detail on a topic or solution.

5. USE PROPER ANCHOR TEXT

When linking to a page, make sure to create descriptive anchor text instead of just adding the full link into your content. A great way to create proper anchor text is to use the primary keyword for the page topic you are linking to. This will help Google understand what that page is about and give the customer insight into what they will be clicking on.

In the example below, we created a blog post about bounce rate optimization, and in one of the steps, we linked to another blog post that can dive deeper into video optimization. The link uses the anchor text "Get your videos to rank on Google."

8. Add videos to your content

Another great way to keep users from exiting your page is to give them something to do and what is better than watching a video? A video can be an extremely powerful piece of content to enhance your page and even your rankings. If you are adding a video make sure it is:

- Relevant to the primary keyword of the page
- Structured properly to include video schema
- 30 seconds – 3 minutes long
- Embedded straight on your page and not just a clickable link
- Checkout our blog post on the exact steps you need to take to get your videos to rank on Google.

Anchor Text

6. LINK PAGE TOPICS

When implementing internal linking, make sure every page on your site is linked in some way. Make it a priority to go through your site and find the common categories to link together. In the graphic below, you can see the internal linking structure. The more posts that are related to a specific category and are linked together, the more Google will think you are an expert about that topic and will show your posts more often in organic search results or a Featured Snippet.

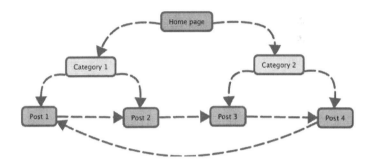

7. LINK TO HIGH CONVERTING PAGES

All the steps we listed above are essential aspects of internal linking, but you should use this SEO technique strategically to get results. If your goal is to convert customers into purchasing a product or signing up for a software demo, link to pages where you want to drive the customer to complete an action.

Also, understand what is converting on your site. A great way to do this is to complete an analysis of your website and determine the top 3-5 converting pages that lead to a conversion or customer action. Once you know what pages those are, strategically link to those pages where the topic/categories are similar.

This will improve your organic rankings and send the customer through the path that will eventually lead to them completing an action you want.

Internal Linking: What NOT to do

Here are a few tips and tricks about what NOT to do with your internal linking strategy:

- Don't use phrases like "Click Here"
- Don't link more than one sentence
- Don't use exact match anchor text
- Don't point all your links to the same page
- Don't force content just to get links
- Don't use "rel=nofollow" on internal links.

Chapter 18 Review

1. Did you add an internal link to every appropriate page on your website?

2. What primary content groups did you use when adding your internal links?

CHAPTER 21

MULTI-LOCATION OPTIMIZATION

Author: Roger Bryan - Growth Foundry

If your business has multiple locations, you need to have a specific page created for each location that includes all the details. Below is the 5-step process to setup multi-location schema markup using the WP Store Locator plugin.

1. Add "WP Store Locator" plugin

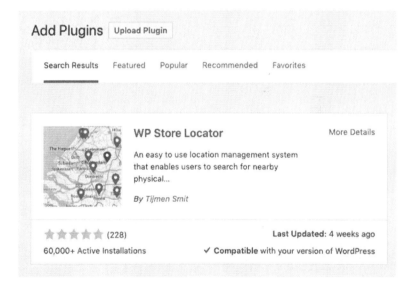

2. Go to Store Locator "settings"

3. Click "Add New Store" – Although it says store, you can use this feature for any business location

4. Create your "store"

Store Details

Location   Opening Hours   Additional Information

Address: *   [_____]

Address 2:   [_____]

City: *   [_____]

State: [_____]

Zip Code: [_____]

Country: *   United States

Latitude: [_____]

Longitude: [_____]

Add in your page name which could be "Your Business + Location" and then scroll down until you find "Store Details." Enter the details about your business location (this information is what you will be marking up).

Next, add content to your page that is specific to that business location and publish.

Pro Tip: When creating this page, look at what you can markup in the structured data markup tool and make sure to add as much information you can markup as possible when determining what to include on the page.

5. Markup your page

Follow the structured data markup guide above and markup your web page using the "local business" as your data type.

Repeat with other business locations

Continue creating storefronts and marking up your location pages until you have created a page with location schema for each of your business locations.

OPTIMIZING LOCAL LANDING PAGES

Below are a few tips to help you optimize your local landing pages:

- Make sure you include the city and state in your landing page title

- Have quality local inbound links

- Have your primary keyword in title tag and meta description

- Include your local business map embed on the landing page

- Have your business name, address, and phone number (NAP) listed

- Include your business hours (if possible)

- Add a paragraph that talks about local attractions and includes multiple links to local authoritative sites

- Include a list of services for that specific location

- Add reviews and star ratings for your product or service

- Include a strong and clear call to action

CHAPTER 22

OPTIMIZING FOR VOICE SEARCH

Author: Roger Bryan - Growth Foundry

HOW IS VOICE SEARCH CHANGING THE WAY WE APPROACH SEO?

Voice search isn't new. As early as 2008, technology has been experimenting with voice activated assistants. Starting in 2010, this technology became more a part of our lives as Siri (from Apple) was born (April 28, 2010 – yes, she really does have a birthday). In late 2014, Amazon launched Alexa, which triggered the massive expansion of voice search that we're seeing today.

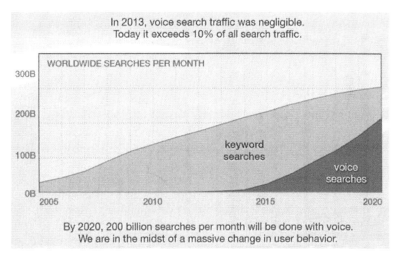

From: http://www.mdconnectinc.com/medical-marketing-insights/search-engine-optimization-the-rise-of-voice-search

By 2020, voice search will more than double from today's volumes. You must be integrating voice search into your search engine optimization strategies.

WHY DO PEOPLE USE VOICE SEARCH?

Personal Assistant and Reminders: We live in a busy world. Everyone can use a little help keeping track of their day-to-day lives.

Entertainment: We are a world on the go. It is easier to say what we want than to open a browser, type, view results, choose the one we want to look at, and then engage. Voice search allows us to say what we want and get it.

Answers to our Questions: One of the first things we learn as children is to ask questions. This is a natural process for us. Voice search taps into our primary understanding of communication and allows us to get the answers we seek.

Local Targeting: When we want something local (a doctor, an urgent care, or a dentist), we can simply ask for one near us and have instant access to the results.

They are on the go: Whether driving, walking, or on the move, voice search allows you to get the answers you need without taking your attention off of what you're already doing.

Elderly: It is much easier for them to ask questions on their phone than it is to search and read the text on their screen.

How to prepare for the shift in voice search?
- Avoid technical content - use conversational tone
- Add a FAQ with common questions to your site
- Use long tail keywords
- Provide direct answers to the most common questions
- Include leading question keywords "who, how, what, where, and when"
- Consider slang in your content efforts

HOW DOES ADOPTING VOICE SEARCH BENEFIT YOUR ORGANIZATION?

Google is now indexing (creating relational values between previously non-relational worlds) more misspellings, slang, and voice inflections.

Pages that ranked for 10 keywords can now rank for 100s or 1000s of keywords if properly optimized.

Organizations that have adopted this strategy early have seen 20-70% increases in search engine optimization traffic.

Meeting the searcher where they are is vital to conversion. Those that adopt a voice search-oriented approach to SEO are more likely to convert visitors that find their site. Think *Questions and Answers* first and you'll win the conversion game.

HOW CAN I IMPROVE MY VOICE SEARCH SEO?

First, review your search console account. Look for queues on what people are searching for most. Then, take the time to do your own voice searches. Do you find your organization when you search? Do the results that come up match with what you would want someone to find?

CHAPTER 23

Video Sitemaps

Author: Roger Bryan - Growth Foundry

To get your video to rank on Google search results, normal SEO efforts are no longer enough. In this chapter, we have mapped out the exact steps you need to take to get your video to rank on Google by creating and submitting video sitemaps easily and effectively.

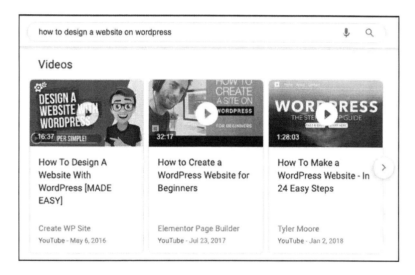

What Are Video Sitemaps?

A Video Sitemap is an extension of the Google sitemap protocol that ties together your video content and the metadata required to get it noticed.

BENEFITS OF A VIDEO SITEMAP

- It makes it clear to Google what your content is
- You have the opportunity to provide a range of details through schema
- Additional presence on video.google.com search
- RAD picture thumbnail, which is a pretty great call to action
- A Video Sitemap is simply a text file that utilizes the sitemap protocol with video specific tags in it. In its simplest form, it would just be a tag that links to the landing page for the video as in this example:

YOUR VIDEO SITEMAP MUST HAVE

- Landing page URL
- Landing page title
- Landing page description
- URL to thumbnail
- Clip ID

HOW TO CREATE AND INDEX YOUR VIDEO SITEMAP

As digital marketers, we are always looking for more efficient ways to complete tasks. Because of this, we have mapped out the easiest way for you to create and index your video sitemap that we have found the most success with.

To correctly create your video sitemap, use the plugin: Yoast Video SEO. This plugin costs $69 per website and is worth every penny to properly implement video SEO with the least amount of effort. Yoast Video SEO is compatible with both Vimeo and YouTube. Below are the exact steps you need to take with Yoast Video SEO.

Step 1: Download and install Yoast Video SEO

Once you have purchased "Yoast Video SEO," install and activate the plugin on your website. Yoast has a great installation guide you can follow if you have any questions.

Step 2: Go to Video SEO Settings in WordPress

Once the plugin has been activated, go to the left-hand side of your WordPress dashboard and click on 'SEO.' The SEO menu will drop down and you will click on 'Video SEO.'

Step 3: General Settings

This section allows you to check the general settings and is where you will find your video sitemap. From here, you can customize the plugin so it only scans items that contain videos when building your video sitemap. Lastly, under indexing, you can force the plugin to index new pages that have not been indexed before (this feature comes in handy in the future after adding multiple videos to your site).

If you currently have no videos on your site, you need to go through the Video SEO checklist above and embed the video before you move onto the next step. If you already have a video embedded on your site, continue to the next step.

Step 4: Visit page with video

Visit the backend of the page on which the video is embedded.

Step 5: Configure Video SEO

Once you are on the page that contains the video, scroll down until you reach the Yoast SEO box. Click the "plug" button that is 4th down on the left to configure your video SEO.

On this screen, you can complete the following things:

1. Add a unique video thumbnail

2. Add the video duration

3. Add relevant tags the video represents

4. Add relevant categories (if your video is on a blog post)

5. Give your video a rating

6. And, if needed, you can mark the video as "not family friendly"

Fill out each section as each element makes up that video sitemap that will be added to your master video sitemap.

Step 6: Index your video

Once you have embedded your video and configured its settings, go back to the general video SEO settings in steps 2 and 3 and force index your video since it was not indexed prior to Yoast Video SEO being activated.

That's it! You have successfully created and indexed your video sitemap for your website. Now each time you embed a video to your website, you can simply go to the Yoast SEO box, enter the video details, and then index via the force index button. Now that you know how to create video sitemaps, we have provided even more video SEO Tips below to help you crush your video rankings.

Video SEO Tips

Optimize your video content by making it sharable and linkable

- Your video should be responsive to mobile viewing (Vimeo does this automatically)

- Upload videos to multiple platforms for max exposure and improved rankings

- Use various keywords in the different places you host the video

- The more text you can attach to your video the more recognition you will receive from search engines

Optimize thumbnails to be engaging

- The more text, images and diverse media on a page, the better it will appear to both the algorithms and potential customers.

- Place the content on an easily accessible page, targeting a term suitable for getting a rich snippet, keeping the video front and center of that page.

- Make sure the page is nicely linked up internally, so you can spread the link equity you're going to get.

- Keep video content unique to the page, giving Google only one option to choose which page should rank for your video.

- Only one video per page

Pro Tip: Any terms including the following keywords are more likely return these rich snippets:

- Tutorial

- Review

- Test

- What is

- How to

- Demonstration

- Explanation

- Video

Only use one video per page so Googlebot does not struggle to pick out an appropriate video to connect with the rich snippets.

THE BEST VIDEO HOSTING PLATFORMS FOR SEO

There are two flagship video hosting platforms that continue to dominate the overall industry: YouTube and Vimeo. Each has their pros and cons and depending on the type of digital marketing you are doing, one of them will be the best fit to jumpstart your video SEO strategy.

YOUTUBE	
PROS	**CONS**
World's most popular video sharing platform	Competitors content or even ads can be displayed near yours
SEO is built in so you can be found for the content of the video	Public content is not as easily controlled or policed
YouTube is owned by Google so often is favored in search results	The network is designed to keep people on site, so people are less likely to visit your website
Annotations can be added within videos to lead people to act (CTA)	Many businesses block YouTube videos internally

YouTube Video SEO Checklist

- ❏ Name video file using the core keyword the video is about

- ❏ Get the video transcribed using rev.com

- ❏ Upload the video to the company's YouTube channel that matches the GMB name

- ❏ Title the video using the core keyword you are trying to rank the video for (Example of keyword: Physical Therapy New York)

- ❏ Add a video description with the following information (URL of page, description of the page, core keyword)

- ❏ Add the proper video tags (any keywords that fall under the page the video will be on)

- ❏ Click on "Advanced Settings" in YouTube and add the date the video was filmed

- ❏ Publish video on YouTube
- ❏ Use the embed link to put the video on the web page
- ❏ Add video schema to the page
- ❏ Make sure video is placed in the video sitemap
- ❏ Share on social channels

VIMEO

VIMEO	
PROS	**CONS**
• No advertising for viewers • Customization of video player (logo, colors, thumbnails etc.) • Can use own domain • Analytics is more detailed • Beautifully designed layout for watching videos • Created for Google to generate a rich snippet • Every Vimeo video embedded on your site contains the thumbnail image and data required for Google to generate a rich video snippet in the organic search results.	• Significantly smaller audience, so less visibility • No Free accounts for business usage (minimum $17 per month) • Restrictions on storage based on plans • Google said to favor YouTube in search results • Vimeo Video SEO Checklist • Name video using the relevant keywords and words the video is based on • Upload video to Vimeo • Choose engaging thumbnail • Give a title and description using keywords and terms to generate rich snippets • Embed video onto your site

VIMEO
<ul><li>For max rank value you want to use the old Vimeo embed code and not the new HTML5</li><li>Click on the "embed" link and then choose "use the old embed code."</li><li>Use a nice large frame on the page (640px by 360px is normally good) and isn't tucked away in a corner, where it will be ignored by a passing visitor.</li><li>Create video XML sitemap so google can index all of your embedded video content</li><li>Resources: TubularInsights.com/Vimeo-Sitemaps</li><li>Resources: TubularInsights.com/How-Video-Sitemaps/</li><li>Submit Video XML sitemap</li><li>Ensure the page the video is on has supporting content, images, and keywords</li></ul>

WHAT IF YOU DON'T HAVE A WORDPRESS WEBSITE?

Google provides a comprehensive guide on how to create your video sitemap with example code, what it needs to include, and what information needs to be in the video sitemap. To create your own video sitemap, follow the Google Video Sitemap guide.

Below is a short checklist you want to follow when creating your own video sitemap

- ❏ Upload videos to proper hosting platform – YouTube or Vimeo (see above for pros and cons of each)

- ❏ Optimize the video according to the instructions outlined in the Vimeo and YouTube checklists

- ❏ Make sure you have the information to meet all Google video required fields

- ❏ Add the master video SEO file to the current live sitemap

- ❏ Submit the sitemap to search console

CHAPTER 24

FEATURED SNIPPETS

Author: Roger Bryan - Growth Foundry

In this chapter, we will outline the six essential steps you need to take to steal your competitor's featured snippet and gain the coveted spot zero in Google organic rankings.

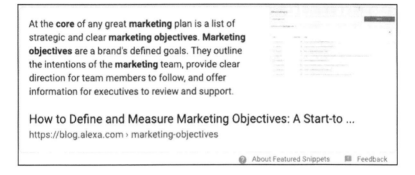

HOW TO OPTIMIZE YOUR PAGE FOR A FEATURED SNIPPET

1. Make sure you are ranking on first page for the primary keyword being used to populate the featured snippet

Your primary keyword does not have to be ranking in the first spot of Google. There are many cases where featured snippets are acquired even when the page is ranking in the 4-10 spot, but you are more likely to take over a featured snippet if you have a higher-ranking page. Specifically, for local SEO marketing, a great example of a primary keyword with a featured snippet is "Local SEO Agency Akron Ohio"

2. Restructure your content to the same format as the current featured snippet

One of the most important aspects of trying to acquire a featured snippet is the way you structure your content. When trying to acquire a featured snippet, you must format your content exactly like the current featured snippet. If the current featured snippet is a list snippet using bullet points, you must use bullet points. Because Google's algorithm already qualifies that format as a featured snippet, you must use the same format.

3. Make sure the structured markup on your site/page is correct

Once you have correctly formatted your page, add structured data that further enhances your content. If the current competitor does not use structured data, this will automatically give you a step above them. Before adding structured data, enter the current competitor's URL that has the featured snippet into Google's Structured Data Testing Tool so you can see how and what your competitors are marking on their page.

Make sure when determining the structured data markup that you are choosing the proper schema for your industry. Schema.org has hundreds of different schema markups, and you can have specific markup from automotive to healthcare.

4. Add headers to break up your page

Another way to organize your page is to add multiple headers to make it easy for Google to scan your page and find the answer that needs to be displayed in the featured snippet. The best headers to use are H1 and H2 but using multiple headers that contain the key question being asked and the primary keyword will help get you closer to obtaining a featured snippet.

5. Add multiple images

Adding relevant images to your web page is critical to obtaining a featured snippet. You want to have 2-5 images overall, and make sure you are adding the correct image alt tags. For maximum effectiveness, you should add a landscape image directly under the content you wish to be the featured snippet. The digital marketing example below shows a great image for "Benefits of Robotic Surgery".

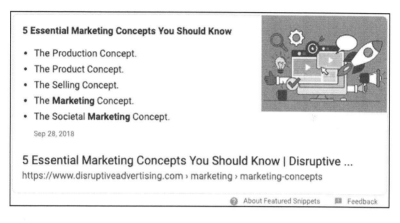

6. Add synonyms of the keywords people would be searching for on the page

When updating your content for the featured snippet, make sure to include synonyms of your primary keyword. One way to optimize your content is to write it using the "people always ask" questions below the featured snippet (see image below). By looking at the questions people are already asking, you can find other featured snippet opportunities and increase the number of synonyms in your content.

People also ask

What are the risks and benefits of bariatric surgery?	∨
Is Bariatric Surgery Necessary?	∨
Does Bariatric Surgery lower BP?	∨
How effective is bariatric surgery?	∨
What are the benefits of gastric sleeve surgery?	∨

Feedback

Once your page has been successfully optimized for a featured snippet, continue to search for other opportunities and keep an eye on the featured snippets you want to take as Google is always searching for better content. You may need to add more keywords and continue to structure until you finally achieve victory.

Below we have outlined more details on featured snippets and have provided resources that will help you find multiple featured snippet opportunities for your website.

BENEFITS OF FEATURED SNIPPETS

- More traffic
- Increased CTR
- More Revenue
- Used for Voice Search

TYPES OF FEATURED SNIPPETS

PARAGRAPH

A paragraph featured snippet has an average of 43 words that give a clearly defined answer to the question being searched and is always followed by a landscape image that accurately relates to the question and answer.

LIST

A list featured snippet has an average of 5-6 list items that uses bullet points or numbers and has under 10 characters per list item.

TABLE

A table snippet shows a table of information with only two rows and three columns.

VIDEO

A video featured snippet takes up the entire space above the fold with an embedded video that the user can watch from Google search results.

TOOLS TO FIND FEATURED SNIPPETS

SEMRUSH

1. Enter your URL into SEMRush
2. Go to Organic Search
3. Go to Positions
4. Click on "Featured Snippets" all the way on the right-hand side of the page
5. This will show you the keywords your competitors are targeting that have given them a featured snippet
6. Next you can click on the blue number, then click on the "view SERP button"
7. This allows you to look at the SERP source to see how the snippet appears on the results page

AHREFS.COM

1. Enter your URL into their site explorer search bar
2. Click on "Organic Keywords."
3. Under the top 10 filter click SERP Features.
4. Click "Featured Snippets" and "All Features."
5. This will reveal all queries that you currently rank for that are in the top 10 of all results that also have a featured snippet.

Remember, this doesn't mean you own the featured snippet; it could be owned by a competitor.

To know what featured snippets you own, you will have to automatically create a spreadsheet and filter the data manually as Ahrefs does not have this feature yet.

WORDS TO USE IN YOUR FEATURED SNIPPET

According to SEMRush, the following keywords are the most common when it comes to featured snippets. View the full breakdown by SEMRush.

QUESTION SNIPPETS

What	Who	Will	How
When	Where	Have	Does
Why	Are	Do	Can
Was	Which	Is	Should

PREPOSITION SNIPPETS

Like	Without	Compared	VS
To	Comparison	Pricing	Versus
With	Compare	Price	Priced
Like	Comparison Snippets		

CHAPTER 25

Google Guarantee Program

Author – Justin Sanger – OMG NATIONAL

Local Services Ads – Google Guaranteed and Screened

Google has introduced a new, dynamic advertising inventory that sits atop its precious search results. It is the source of trusted, just-in-time answers. **Local Services Ads (LSA)** form the ad layer that delivers these results. I call it the "trust layer." The ads look and act differently than any results that we are familiar with as search marketers.

In this bonus chapter, we will begin to unpack Google LSA and the **Google Guaranteed** for Home Services and **Google Screened** for Professional Services programs. In doing so, we will address the impact that these advertising programs will have on the local search landscape of the future.

In 2014, Google My Business was born, and Google's leadership in local search was unrivaled. It was then that Google began asking itself broader questions around the implications of directing trillions of dollars in off-line local transactions. For the first time, Google was seriously asking itself about its responsibility for the safety and security of its users that find businesses on its results.

By then, Google was speaking in terms of "micro-moments" inside their consumer labs. They were very interested in use-cases for the "right-then," "right-now," "well-advised" user. It knew that the manifestation of well-advised moments in local meant trust.

Google had a business ethics consideration before it – a question of what it meant for its users to "trust" its answers. Spam and fraud were consistent concerns on local search results. But the real potential problem was that Google was sending these so-called "service pros" into peoples' homes with families.

In 2015, Google's answer to this historic question would become Advanced Verification for advertisers and Home Services Ads. Five years later, that program has matured significantly. Getting approved now means sitting on the very top of the search results with a green check-mark badge of trust.

Today, Google's Local Services Ads are sweeping across SERPs in the following categories:

Appliance repair services	Architecture services
Bankruptcy law services	Business law services
Carpenter services	Carpet cleaning services
Cleaning services	Contract law services
Countertop services	Criminal law services
Disability law services	DUI law services
Electricians	Event planning services
Estate lawyer services	Family law services
Fencing services	Junk removal services
Financial planning services	Flooring services
Foundations services	Garage door services
HVAC (heating or air conditioning)	Immigration lawyer services
Interior design services	IP law services
Labor law services	Landscaping services
Lawn care services	Litigation law services
Locksmiths	Malpractice law services
Movers	Pest control services
Personal injury lawyers	Photography services
Plumbers	Real estate law services
Real estate services	Roofers
Siding services	Tax law services
Tax services	Traffic law services
Tree services	Videography services
Water damage services	Window cleaning services
Window repair services	

GOOGLE'S LOCAL BADGE OF TRUST

The Google Badge is the centerpiece of the trust layer, and is a designation that is earned by a business owner within the distinct Guaranteed and Screened programs. The badge means that the business has passed the approval process and is eligible for running LSA as a Google trusted business.

BENEFITS OF THE BADGE

- Take advantage of advertising units that display on the top of Google's search results
- Upgrade your business status online as a trusted, Guaranteed, or Screened provider
- Maintain an LSA business profile which includes vital information about your business
- Mitigate risk by paying for leads, not clicks, on a cost-per-call basis
- Demonstrate your commitment of quality, safety, and trustworthiness to the communities you serve

GOOGLE GUARANTEE

The Google Guaranteed program now covers most home service categories. The badge for Guaranteed providers signifies the business has been verified and Google backs the services.

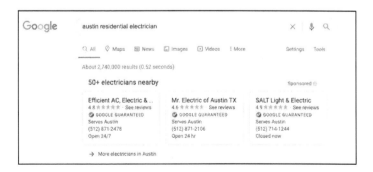

Google may refund their users the amount paid for the service provided by a Google Guarantee business. The limit of lifetime coverage for claims is $2,000, but services must be booked through Google Local Services.

GOOGLE SCREENED

In 2020, Google launched Screened for Professional Services providers. The groundbreaking program initially hit the scene for lawyers, financial planners, and real estate agents. At the time of writing, the lawyer selection has expanded to support seventeen different job categories for lawyers alone. The Screened offerings will likely continue to evolve.

The Google Screened badge conveys that the background and professional credentials of the provider have been verified. The inventory is starting to sweep the nation with hungry professional services businesses who want to tell their community and prospects how trustworthy they are atop important keyword searches on Google.

BADGE APPROVAL PROCESS

To qualify for the badge, service pros undergo an examination that we as marketers, technologists, and business owners may find uncomfortable. On the other hand, if you are a user on Google and in need of a trusted pro, you will likely find the qualification process quite comforting.

Getting the badge is a success for a business. The badge is a symbol of trust that is transportable. In fact, Google has already publicly flirted with plans for business owners to be able to display their badge on their GMB page. The badge is a designation that will live with the business, irrespective of how much they use LSA.

Getting to the top of the SERPs is important, but first, you must be prepared for the following off-line approval processes:

- Personal identity and background checks for authorized representatives of the business and any "field workers" that interact with the customer in a transactional setting.

- Business status check relating to litigation history, judgements, and liens filed against it.

- General liability insurance certificate submissions, in certain categories, with variable minimums.

- Checks to ensure that the businesses hold appropriate licenses at the appropriate federal, state, county, and city levels.

At present, the entire process of getting approved for the badge is time consuming, tedious, and frustrating. Google relies on multiple third parties throughout the application process.

LOCAL SERVICES ADS (LSA)

LSA is a closed-loop advertising system. Its self-regulating dataflow gives Google precise control around its ad serving rules. To power the closed-loop advertising inventory, Google asks its advertisers to provide the insights that drives its decisions.

This data helps Google understand what prospect phone calls that they should send to what advertisers at what time of the day to get the best result for its users.

LSA's base taxonomy is an industry category (lawyer) to job category (family lawyer) to job type (adoption) to keyword ontology.

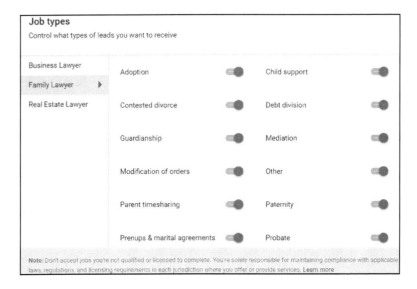

Job type keywords combine with service areas and ad schedule to serve as foundational ad serving rules.

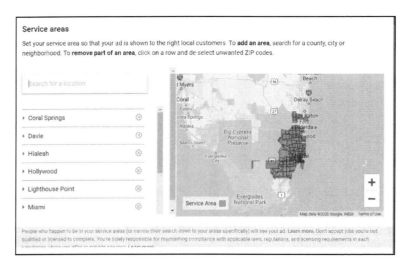

LSA COST-PER-CALL PRICING

Google's LSA cost-per-call inventory is an extraordinary advertising pricing achievement. It started as a fixed cost-per-call model but has quickly matured. Now, an AdWords like open-bidded model has arrived.

Invariably, Google wants to make the process simple for advertisers by having businesses tell them how many leads they want per month at what times, so Google can recommend a budget.

How do you want to bid?

⦿ **Maximize leads** Recommended

Choose this option to let Google set your bid and get you the most leads for your budget.

○ **Set max per lead**

Choose this option to manually set your own bid, the maximum cost you want to pay for a lead.

How well your ad does depends on your reviews, customer service and more. Learn more

---

The cost per call will vary depending on location, business category type, and lead channel (message or phone lead). LSA ads focus on an average weekly budget based on a target number of leads. Calls that are not valid leads are easily disputed and credited.

Google's newest feature allows for Message leads priced at half that of a call.

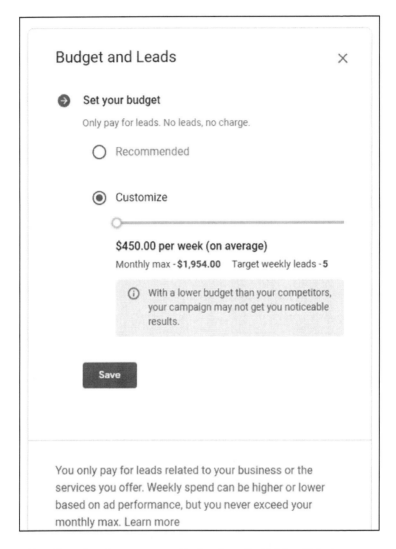

For Google, the concept of what is a "valid lead" is important. Their rules include a text message or email, a voicemail from the customer, the answering of a phone call and the proceeding conversation with a prospect, a response to the customer's message, and a booking request from the customer. Leads that Google often credits include LSA induced contacts that requested a job or location not on your business profile

The LSA Profile

The LSA Profile plays a critical role as a standalone landing page, unlike any other "profile" within the Google Local display environment. The profile is the most stable and rich view of a single-location business display within Google's ecosystem.

The LSA Dashboard

The LSA Dashboard is available online and through the mobile app. The Dashboard allows advertisers to organize and sort their leads, dispute calls, view spend and volume metrics, customize aspects of the profile, control ad serving conditions, and view billing. The mobile app becomes critical to providers on-the-go.

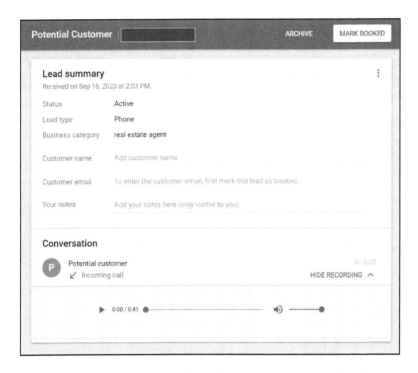

Optimization means teaching Google what type of calls you want and when you want to receive them. Google counts on its advertisers to deliver inputs into its closed-loop system that affect whether your LSA ads show up. But it is their review score, responsiveness to customers, the proximity to users' locations, and hours of operation that matter most.

The LSA dashboard is also a leads management and performance reporting tool.

For LSA, it is important to conduct ongoing analysis of call trends, including the review of unanswered and archived or disputed calls. Since calls generated through the program affect Job Types and Location targeting decisions, they should be listened to carefully to avoid non-relevant calls in the future.

GETTING LSA PROFILE REVIEWS

Google Reviews grow in importance in the LSA environment. The review process is segmented from the broader GMB review process. The intent of the reviews on LSA is to inform Google as to the efficacy of its ad serving, as much as it is to inform users as to the efficacy of a business.

THE GOOGLE REVIEW LINK

Google provides advertisers with a Google review link, and providers are encouraged to share the link directly with customers.

It is critical that advertisers mark their leads as booked when closed. When this is accomplished, Google asks for authorization to send the advertiser's review link to the consumer. This is amongst the most important signals that Google could receive to inform their ad serving rules and benefit your program.

Google can ask for a review
Share a few details to help Google ask on your behalf

This job was received on Sep 16, 2020 at 02:03 PM.

Customer email address*   Customer name*

Job type
Unspecified   ▼   Service location

* Required Field

☐ I confirm the customer agreed to receive this email

CANCEL   SEND

GOOGLE VERIFIED REVIEWS

The closed-loop system of Google LSA rewards advertisers with a "Google Verified" label for reviews obtained from users who were sent the LSA review link specifically through the dashboard.

CONCLUSION

Google's Local Services Ads are unlike anything we have seen in search. They involve the advertiser in progressive new ways. LSAs ask the business to continually produce qualitative signs that enable the Google advertising system to learn, while delivering trust to users.

The requirements for the program mean that many small businesses simply will not qualify. Other issues stem from the advanced functioning of the inventory itself and the advertiser's ability to feed it what it needs to work for them. At the same time, the position and purpose of the inventory means that advertisers and users alike will have a hard time ignoring it.

Regardless of the challenges, Google has managed to create a final trust layer in local search that incorporates conditions and interactions which provide confidence to Google users in the right-then, right-now, well-advised micro-moment in local discovery.

All the while, Google is asking more of the advertiser – to respond to business inquiries in a timely manner, provide clear pricing and service integrity, be safe, and yes, "be kind" to keep your good standing in the program.

Advertisers are now held to account for unlikely standards of quality. LSA will change the game in local advertising. Google's focus on user safety is a clear indictment on advertiser integrity.

LSA will define our decade in local search.

ABOUT JUSTIN SANGER

Justin is a pioneer and leader in the local marketing technology industry. Recognized for his innovations in the space, he has over 20 years' experience creating products, deploying teams, and building markets in the local advertising arena. He is currently an Equity Investor and Chief Revenue Officer at OMG National, a leading local marketing products and platform provider.

Contributor: Ajay Gaikwad, Lead LSA Analyst, OMG National

OMG National specializes in the Google Guaranteed and Screened Programs and the management of Local Services Ads for businesses. For readers to take advantage of OMG's special LSA - Trust Pack offer go to www.OMGNational.com/seo90.

Section 4
Making it Happen

CHAPTER 26

TOOLS YOU SHOULD USE

CHOOSING THE RIGHT TECHNOLOGY

Technology plays a critical role in any data-driven marketing campaign. You need to have a house for all of your data and systems to process that data.

There are thousands to choose from, but I'm just going to give you some of the top choices that I've worked with in the past.

ANALYTICS, DATA MANAGEMENT AND REPORTING

AgencyAnalytics (AA): AA is a great tool for tracking all of your data in one easy-to-use dashboard. You can create accounts for each of your clients and track their keyword rankings, run site audits, connect all analytics and social tools, and even give your clients their own real-time marketing dashboard. Our favorite feature of AA is the reporting capabilities, which allow you to create gorgeous reports to send to your client without much work. AA has pre-made templates that work great for any campaign, and you can customize them to provide exactly what your client wants to see.

RESEARCH AND COMPETITIVE ANALYSIS

SEMRush: SEMRush is one of our favorite tools for competitive analysis. SEMRush allows you to run any website and find out what keywords they rank for, how much they spend on paid advertising, what their online presence looks like, and much more. SEMRush is also a great tool to run site audits, track keyword rankings, and complete a backlink audit. Lastly, it allows you to enter your site and it will show you the entire SEO competitive landscape, so you know exactly what keywords to focus on to outrank your competition.

Page Optimizer Pro (POP): POP is our go-to tool when optimizing a page against competition. POP allows you to enter in your website, a set of core keywords, and top five competitors and will analyze all sites and ranks and give you a checklist of items you need to do to get that landing page to rank above your competitors.

Ubersuggest: This is another great tool to determine what keywords should be the focus of your marketing campaign efforts. It's extremely user friendly and lets you enter in multiple keywords to determine how much volume and value they would bring to your site.

MOZ: MOZ is similar to SEMRush and allows you to run backlink audits, site audits, track keywords, and complete competitor and keywords research. We like using multiple tools for keyword research because you can find varying results.

aHRefs: Similar to MOZ and SEMRush, aHRefs is another SEO tool that allows you to complete competitor and keyword research. It can show you what pages your competitors have that are driving the most traffic. You can enter a keyword and see what recent content pieces have had the most traction and much more.

Keyword Planner Tool: Google AdWords has a great keyword tool for when you are just getting started. You must have an AdWords account to use it, but if you don't have one, you can make a test account to access the keyword planner. We love this tool because it allows you to type in multiple keywords at once and will suggest better keywords based on search volume, CPC, and more.

SCHEMA TOOLS

Google structured data testing tool: Structured data has become increasingly important in any SEO strategy, and the best tool we have found to test schema is Google's structured data testing tool. This tool allows you to enter the URL of any webpage to see if your schema has any issues, and if so, what issues and how to fix them.

INTEGRATION TOOLS

Zapier: Being able to integrate different data sources to provide your company with automation is one of the key factors to running an efficient marketing campaign. Zapier allows you to send data to different platforms, emails, spreadsheets, Google Docs, and much more, so you never have to manually copy and paste data from one platform to the other.

PROJECT AND CAMPAIGN MANAGEMENT

Asana: Our team manages all of their campaigns through Asana, which allows you to view each individual's list of tasks to complete and create project boards for each client so that all the information is organized. We love Asana because it can give you a macro overview of your business by showing full calendars, timelines, and workflows of your entire company's tasks. It can also show individual workflows and how much time is dedicated to each client or task.

Trello: Trello is an alternative to Asana and works best for smaller teams or big picture items. Trello allows you to create amazing project boards where you can drag and drop tasks with ease. For independent marketers or small teams, Trello can be a great alternative to Asana.

Slack: Our team uses Slack in conjunction with Asana to manage all clients on a daily basis. Slack allows you to chat with team members quickly and efficiently, so you don't have to waste time sending emails back and forth.

Google Sheets: Our marketing agency uses Google Sheets multiple times per day. We use them to track all weekly and monthly reporting data, outline research and KPI's for each client, and to send all of our completed tasks in Asana to Google Sheets so we can flow them into Agency Analytics and provide the client with a monthly list of tasks we did on their website without ever having to click a button.

CHAPTER 27

Setting Goals and Managing Campaigns

Marketing will always be an ongoing part of your business, so it is necessary to set goals and manage your marketing campaigns effectively to ensure success.

Goals need a target number

- Improve rank (from what to what)
- Improve traffic (by how much +20% in 90 days)
- Improve conversions (what is the 30/90 target number)

Always use KPIs when creating your goals

- Your goal analysis needs to include: We are currently here (data), we want to be here (goal data), this is how we will get there (strategy)
- There must be goals set for organic AND paid. If you have a client doing both organic and paid marketing, you must create two goals
- Rank Types (bad to good)
- Does not rank
- Traction (11-49)
- First Page (4-10)
- Target (1-3)

CREATING YOUR GOALS

When creating goals, first go to the KPI spectrum and review each data point to determine where effort needs to be applied

If rank is causing low impressions, traffic, conversion, etc., then your goal should be focusing on rank.

Example: 80% of keywords are ranking in traction spots 11-49

Your goal must also include the data point for the month prior and the data point you are working towards.

Example: Current visibility score is 36% and average rank is 24.6

Lastly, your goal needs to include the strategy of how to obtain the goal.

Example: Add keyword-rich FAQ's to low-ranking pages and drive internal and external content to the page

USING GOALS WHEN ANALYZING WEEKLY REPORTS

Each week when you are completing weekly analysis, make sure to add the goal into the analysis and map out the progress from the week prior that was related to the goal.

In the analysis, you have to add a "progress" section with updated data related to the goal to ensure the data is improving each week.

If the data is not improving for two weeks, you need to dive into why the progress is not being made.

If any tasks become apparent during the weekly report analysis, add them as tasks for the week

COMPARING GOALS TO OPEN TASKS

Each Monday after you complete your weekly reports, complete an audit of open tasks for each client

Make sure each task is in relation to the goal.

If the task would NOT help reach the goal, consider pushing the due date or closing the task

USING GOALS TO SHOW CLIENTS YOUR PROGRESS

Your weekly analysis will include a section titled "progress" where you should be mapping out the data from the week prior and see if it is improving.

This progress should be discussed during each client call.

When monthly reports are complete, you must report on the progress in relation to the goal to ensure quarterly goals are being met.

KPI SPECTRUM

Rank KPI's		Search KPI's		Traffic KPI's	
Avg. Rank	Visibility Score	Impressions	CTR	Users	Sessions
9.6	86.7%	1,476	1.5%	345	276

Site KPI's		Conversion KPI's	
Time on Site	Bounce Rate	Conversion Rate	Conversions
1:20	73%	1.76%	24

Ironing out your marketing strategy is one of the first steps to salvaging your situation.

Doing something without a vision or a proper plan is like building a product that no one wants. You not only waste your precious time and resources building it, but also end up disappointed at its impending failure. And you may even lose your volition to continue, so it is absolutely important to create a structure that involves setting up specific marketing goals and objectives for your business. Yours may be a fledgling startup that aspires to prepare the world for the future or an established organization with its roots already clung tight to the earth. But without a solid marketing plan that defines a set of objectives and higher goals, your business will become vulnerable. Today, the importance of marketing in business success trumps everything else that was relevant a decade ago – all thanks to the rise of the internet.

MARKETING GOALS AND OBJECTIVES

Have you ever heard the story of a merchant who sold demand to create a higher demand? He would sell vases of flowers in the market area of his hometown. The vases were hand-crafted and so beautiful that anyone would buy them to add some jazz to their living room. Through word of mouth, the vases' popularity grew quickly, and so did their demand in the marketplace.

But no one realized that the merchant's primary product was not the vase but the flowers, which would wither away in less than seven days. He sold the vases to create a constant and never-ending demand for flowers, which would help his business flourish even when he ran out of vases.

In this fictional anecdote of an entrepreneur marveling at his job, the marketing goal is that of creating a never-ending demand for something that he can supply. And he reaches that goal through a series of objectives – getting the vases made, their logistics, marketing them, and maintaining their popularity. The objectives, when completed one by one, lead to satisfaction of the business goal.

Essentially, a marketing goal is the higher point of a journey that you reach through target-specific objectives set up as per the needs and conditions of your business. An online store selling smartphones can have the goal of reaching 100,000 visitors per month. Here, some of the common marketing objectives will be:

- Setting up the website
- Optimizing the content for success in organic and paid search to establish online visibility
- Setting up the e-store and a secure payment gateway to reinforce trust among consumers
- Creating and running a blog to further improve visibility.

A series of objectives typically lead to the achievement of a goal. But how do they differ exactly? Where do these marketing objectives come from? And what should you pay more attention to? What is the importance of a marketing plan in business? Why are goals and objectives important? The answers to these questions are a bit tricky, as you will find out.

All of which brings us to the question of how.

How can a manager be in control of all these parameters without losing focus? From SERP ranks to conversion rate to optimizing content to monitoring advertisement spend and revenue – where do you move your head without causing lapses in the cycle? Through the use of technology, of course.

ACHIEVING MARKETING OBJECTIVES WITHOUT BREAKING A SWEAT

One of the oldest concepts of defining goals and objectives is to go the SMART way. And it is relieving to find that it is still as relevant as it was when it was first adopted. Together with assistance from online tools and resources, you can easily minimize your load when you think about marketing goals and objectives. Here's how…

SMART GOALS

SMART goals are those that provide you with an easy way to ensure that you start running in the morning and don't get lost on the way back home. When you are creating your goals, make sure they are:

Sensible – Have real expectations and be specific in what you're striving for (e.g., ranking on page 1 for a competitive keyword as compared to ranking at #1 early in the campaign)

Measurable – You must have a way to determine if your efforts are successful (e.g., SERP monitoring, automatic reporting mechanisms, etc.)

Achievable – Stay within the realm of possibilities (e.g., outranking a Wikipedia article as opposed to a website with a domain authority of thirty)

Realistic – Avoid setting objectives that are too difficult to accomplish (e.g., outranking a Wikipedia article which is at #1)

Time-specific – Make sure that you frame the goals within a reasonable amount of time. Give yourself a definite date to keep yourself motivated (e.g., 100 citations in three months.)

By applying this formula, you will be able to create smart Local SEO objectives and goals that are not only attainable but also profitable.

CHAPTER 28

FINDING PEOPLE TO DO THE WORK FOR YOU

There are a few different ways to find people to do your SEO Work for you. You can hire an agency, hire a freelancer, or try to find a local or remote intern.

Hiring a Local SEO Agency is the all-in approach. It allows you to hire professionals in the field who will handle every single aspect of the marketing campaign, so all you have to do is see the extra customers and online traffic flowing into your business.

A freelancer will handle some of the marketing efforts for your business but will not be a dedicated account manager for all of your marketing needs.

An intern will allow you to have someone in person, but most interns will have to go through a steep learning curve just learning the ins and outs of your campaign.

HIRE A LOCAL SEO AGENCY

Hiring a Local SEO Agency can seem like a simple process, but you want to make sure it is the right fit for your business and worth the monthly payment you will be giving them.

1. CLEARLY DEFINE YOUR SEO GOALS TO BRING TO THE TABLE

Doing this allows business owners to determine if the marketing agency is reaching their goals and can help them understand the value the agency brings to a business. Often people make the mistake of outsourcing marketing to an agency and then sitting back, hoping the agency tells them if it's working. A clearly-defined goal allows an agency to understand what they are trying to accomplish to make a business successful.

2. CHOOSE A MARKETING FIRM THAT IS SOLIDLY BACKED BY DATA

The easiest way to do this is to find a local search engine optimization (SEO) agency. Most local SEO Agencies will do some preliminary work for you, such as setting up a dashboard that integrates all of your data to provide a clear picture of your current marketing efforts. They will also share reports about your competitors using data that shows who and where your competitors are ranking and provide action items on what needs to happen with your website to beat the competition based on the data they have collected. As we have mentioned in previous chapters, you are not competing with Google when it comes to SEO; you are competing against your competitors and the efforts they have implemented in the past. As long as the agency you hired can do better SEO than your competitors, you will win regardless of what Google does.

3. FIND AN AGENCY THAT IS GOOD AT WHAT THEY DO AND HAS HISTORICAL RESULTS

I always recommend finding a firm that specializes in your space. For example, some SEO firms specialize in working with dentists, lawyers, or multi-location organizations. The people that work with attorneys, lawyers, or dentists have a special skill set, know where to put content, which pages to optimize, and a better understanding of the overall strategy. Ultimately, SEO is a traffic source that must be converted into customers, and the conversion path can vary depending on the industry. For example, our organization works in different vertices, including healthcare SEO, nonprofit SEO, multi-location SEO, small and midsize business SEO, and local SEO.

4. MAKE SURE THE AGENCY YOU ARE HIRING HAS A PROVEN TRACK RECORD

A great way to confirm this to get case studies of clients that directly relate to the type of business that you have.

5. Direct the Buying Process Instead of Allowing the Agency to Dictate the Flow

Go in with a list of questions that you have for the agency. Make sure to ask beyond the simple questions of "How much does it cost?" and "How fast will you get it done?" Ask the questions that let you know they understand your business, your competition, and your niche. The sales process begins with an initial phone call. If they try to sell you on the first call, that is usually a sign they do not have the most robust understanding of your business.

We begin with an initial consultation with our clients, answer some questions, and understand the marketing goals. Next, we do some research on the website, competitors, space, and schedule a phone call to review the marketing landscape. Lastly, we integrate all of the data into one of our dashboards to ensure the client has all the proper marketing tools like Google Analytics and Google Search Console in place, properly structured website and run a full site and competitive audit. Using all of that information, we show the marketing opportunities, review the steps we will take to improve upon the current business, and discuss the time frame to reach the goal.

Depending on the industry or customer, it can happen a little faster. We've talked to some people who have come to us via a referral from someone in the industry just once or twice. They understand that we know what we are doing and ask us upfront if we can solve their problem – and we make it happen. But in the majority of cases, we like to do our research and go through the data, so we don't find ourselves in a situation where the client doesn't have the defined end result that they're seeking. Although you're willing to spend the money, you might have unrealistic expectations, or we could set unrealistic expectations by not doing our proper research.

6. Clearly Define Your Budget and Your Timeframe

I leave this as the last tip because if you try to do this first, you might have an unrealistic expectation of how much work truly goes into having proper marketing for your business. If you say, "I want to rank number one for a keyword that has 100,000 visits a month in 90 days, and I've got $1,000 per month budget," well, take that $3,000, 90 days, and burn it because that's probably what's going to happen. Once you've talked to the agency and set your goal, let them tell you what it should cost and how much effort and time it will take. Rely on the agency's experience. We recommend talking to a couple of different agencies to tell you what it's going to cost.

Marketing doesn't happen overnight. Plan on spending six months to get traction and start seeing some traffic and maybe some conversion. Decide then whether you feel like the price point is acceptable.

By following these tips, you won't go into a conversation with unrealistic expectations. I have talked to people who have a national eCommerce business, want to rank for a hyper-competitive keyword, and only want to spend $1,000 a month when it would cost $5,000 a month and take 12 months to reach their goal of keyword domination. Unfortunately, we have to tell those people, "Best of luck," and walk away because the expectations are too high, and if we took on the client, neither of us would be happy with the results.

These six steps to choosing a good agency will help you find a company that will do everything in their power to drive traffic and conversion for your business.

Things to be Wary of When Hiring an Agency

Next, I want to discuss a few things you should consider when hiring an Agency.

1. Avoid Agencies that Use Third Parties for Sales

Several agencies outsource sales to third parties because their only goal is to close. These sales reps have done zero research, rarely have a marketing background, and their main goal is to get your money. These same agencies normally use a "one size fits all" cookie cutter checklist to deliver results. They don't care if it doesn't work because they've already been paid. You don't want an agency that uses the same strategy for everyone and only focuses on aggressive sales tactics.

2. Avoid Cookie-Cutter Agencies

Be very wary of the cookie cutters. These agencies say things like, "Every SEO client is the same. I have a strategy that ranks someone every time." Because of the complex landscape of SEO marketing, this is impossible. The niches and the industries are so specific and getting quality links in every space requires work and knowledge.

3. Avoid Inexpensive SEO Agencies

You also want to be careful of inexpensive SEO agencies. Not only will they not deliver, but they often can bring harm to your business. We have taken on clients who hired an inexpensive developer or firm on Fiverr or Upwork, and the first thing we notice when we get into their website is there is a 40% toxic link ration. By the time we clean that up, get it out of the website's system, and add in quality links, they are six months behind where they should be because they tried to go cheap. If you are not in a competitive space, which is rare, some cheap work can get results, but you're always at risk of being penalized by Google, which is extremely easy to have happen.

4. Be Wary of Using a Firm Only Because It's Local

A prospective client in California said, "Hey, you know what? I want to go with this firm because they're right down the street and I want to have them close." I understand the safety net that occurs when you think you are choosing a local business. However, if they do not follow the six tips that we talked about above, it doesn't matter if they are closer. It will not be the quality work your business needs to increase success. For example, one of my good friends runs an agency out of Salt Lake City that is one of the best SEO firms in the legal space. If the local law firm chooses a local agency, they probably would not have even 20% of the results the Salt Lake City agency could have provided. Anytime.

5. You Must do Your Research

If you don't do your research, talk to multiple agencies, ask questions, set goals, and come to the table ready, the only person to blame when your campaign doesn't work is you. You must make the proper informed buying decision.

6. Walk Away from Agencies that Say They Can Provide Overnight Rankings

If an Agency gives you instant leads only from SEO, run away from them (unless those leads are coming from a Facebook ad campaign). It could come from AdWords campaigns. There are many things that you can do to get instant leads, but SEO is typically not one of them. It takes time to gain that traction. If an agency says they will do your search engine submissions, ask them what the hell that means (because it doesn't actually mean anything).

7. Run if an Agency Says They Will Generate "X" Number of Backlinks

Backlinks are not about numbers; they are about quality over quantity. If they give you ROI projections, question them on how they came to that metric. For example, we are confident that we can do that properly, but only after doing our research, being integrated in all of your data, and understanding your current conversions and revenue streams. If we don't integrate into your data and know that you're getting 134 conversions and generating $26,000 a week from that, how can we give you an ROI projection? So, be cautious of someone that gives you an ROI projection without having gone through all of your data and being able to articulate that.

Also, avoid people that talk about scraping, spinning, bulk link building, bad press releases, or other things that you want to avoid.

If you follow these rules, you'll typically find a good agency. Now, I want to make it simple for you. I didn't write this book just to write it. We believe that we are a great agency. If you're in the healthcare, nonprofit, a multi-location or franchise, or you run a local services business, we can help. Now, there will be some verticals in the local services business, like dentists or lawyers, that we might refer you out to someone else. But if you run a plumbing company, an HVAC company, a contractor, many other things in the local space, technology companies (like a Microsoft Partner), there's tons that we can do, and multiple case studies we can give you to show you what we've done in the past.

How to Hire a Freelancer

1. Post a job listing to UpWork

2. Create new job post

3. Add the Job Title

4. Make job title ESP

5. Be specific: <skill based title + outcome>

6. Include the outcome you want from the person you are seeking to hire

7. Find proper job category

8. Use UpWorks Tool to map the best category

9. Add business description

10. Have an intro about the business

Enfusen is a local marketing company that provides SEO and Lead Generation Services. We work with both local and national clients but focus mainly on local SEO.

1. **MAP OUT THE *EXACT* GOAL YOU WANT TO ACHIEVE FROM HIRING SOMEONE**

   - Use Kanban Project Management Software
   - Here is the issue from a user's perspective
   - Here is what we believe is wrong and the issues that are caused by it being wrong
   - Here is what life would look like after the issue is fixed (how should the asset work)
   - Here is the timeline we have to fix this issue

2. **PROVIDE SPECIFIC DETAILS**

   - What have we done to try to fix this?
   - Copies of any reports or previous conversations
   - Direct them to the website where the issue is with exact detail on what they should be seeing (as the problem)

3. **MAP OUT THE *EXACT* ISSUE YOU ARE TRYING TO SOLVE WITH DETAIL**

   - Provide any necessary resources or information
   - Craft specific questions that will help eliminate bad applicants (interview questions)
   - Ask them to detail the problem back to you to show they understand the issue
   - Ask them to explain how they will approach fixing the issue to show they have a plan
   - Ask them for an estimated timeframe/budget so there is agreement in advance on cost
   - Ask them to explain how the asset will work after they are done with their work
   - Ask them to provide samples of work that relate directly to the asset you're working on

4. **TRY AN INTERN**

   - Many local universities or local research organizations have intern programs that you can tap into.

CHAPTER 29

Converting Traffic Into Leads

Converting visitors to leads may sound like a difficult concept, but it's quite simple when you follow a few tried and true suggestions from marketing professionals. While you may not always follow these steps in order or need to complete each one for every client, knowing that these methods work – and are available – can be very helpful. There are seven things to remember when converting visitors to your site into leads, and in turn, into lasting customers.

1. Know Your Target Audience

This involves more than simply deciding what types of people you want to appeal to with your site and your product offerings. To be effective with this aspect of lead conversion, you'll also need to know these people (or businesses) more thoroughly. To craft sites and products or services, focus on what these leads will want and need. By appealing to the intricacies of individual audience members, you'll likely be more successful in grabbing and keeping their attention over time. While no two leads will have the same needs or expectations, setting yourself up for success by finding the right ways to appeal to them is essential.

2. Have a Defined Offer

Having a defined offer will show visitors that you can provide them with a specific product or service that is beneficial to them. This offer doesn't need to be a laid-out plan for a particular marketing campaign, (because this will need to be personalized to individual leads and clients). Instead, it should highlight that you, as a business, will be able to meet their needs, no matter what it is that they require. This offer can be simple or complex, but it needs to be intriguing because the goal is to entice site visitors to reach out for more information *about* this offer. Individuals and businesses look for ways to boost their SEO and other marketing reach by working with experts, but it's not enough to simply have them look at what you're capable of – they also need to interact.

3. PROVIDE SOCIAL PROOF

Using **social proof** may seem like bragging, but there's nothing wrong with showcasing past (or current) success stories. Providing links or summaries of marketing initiatives that have been proven effective can help boost visitor confidence in your capabilities, especially if these success stories are for organizations that are similar to theirs. Commonly used forms of this proof include case studies, certifications, awards, and proven results. Although you may not want to give out detailed information about past campaigns and past work, showing that your efforts were able to help others by providing numbers and feedback received can go a long way. The more information you can provide in a concise and appealing manner, the better. One important thing to consider is that while it's perfectly fine to let the results speak for themselves, they should still be presented in a logical and relevant way to the scope of your business.

4. INCLUDE A CLEAR CALL TO ACTION (CTA)

A **clear call to action (CTA)** will motivate visitors to take that next step. A CTA is only considered successful when it leads to a conversion. Clicking on a button or a link, making a phone call, or even sending an email are all examples of success. Presenting this CTA on the page in a visible location isn't enough; the CTA must be clear in intent and be compelling. Most visitors won't be inclined to take action unless they know what the result of the action will be. So, even though it may seem like a good idea to focus on the appearance of this CTA (be it a button or a link), you should also focus on the textual content and explanation. Websites may have multiple CTAs, and this is actually recommended because not every portion of a site or every individual page will require the same action to convert. As long as the visitor knows what to do when they click this, you're likely to see the desired results. Determining where to place these CTAs on your website pages ties into knowing your target audience, as well as another step – optimizing your landing pages.

5. OPTIMIZE LANDING PAGES

Making sure **landing pages are optimized** is just as important as having them exist in the first place. There are five things to remember when choosing the best practices for optimizing landing pages.

Be responsive. Since so many people access websites through their mobile devices, it's a good idea to create mobile-friendly pages. That means pages should load quickly and completely no matter what device a visitor is using, feature interactive elements can be easily clicked on and navigated through, and mobile-friendly organization is not overwhelming.

Don't let SEO slip. Even though someone has already chosen to visit your landing page, it's good practice (and can help to keep all pages consistent) to use some of the same keywords, phrases, and even imagery from other locations. If you're taking the time to create the pages and present them to visitors and potential conversions, don't waste an opportunity to appeal to them by stating intent.

Match the pages to user intent. Ensure that your landing pages match the click-through link. While a visit is still good for exposure, many people won't remain on a page long if what they are viewing has nothing to do with what they clicked on… or why. An example of this is an ad for a specific product taking visitors to a page with no connection to the initial ad. Visitors will click for very specific reasons, and if they feel as if their time isn't valued, they'll close the page quickly.

Separating content is good. In some cases, marketing campaigns will use multiple ads or CTAs to draw visitors to the same pages, but in other cases, these individualized ads will need to lead to different landing pages. It's always good practice to make things easy to understand and uncluttered on the page, so while it may take additional time, having separate landing pages can do a lot of good. Not only will visitors feel like they're getting exactly what they're expecting, they will feel as if you've tailored the site-visit experience specifically to them and their needs.

Don't let your visitors slip away. It doesn't matter how many clicks you have that bring people to your landing pages - the key is **keeping** them there until they've made a decision and understand what you're offering them. Though it may seem like a good idea to add in different links and buttons to other pages, that can be detrimental to your overall efforts. Whenever possible, limit distractions and keep visitors focused on exactly what you're trying to tell them with a single page.

6. Capture Information

Finding a way to capture information is important. There are several different ways to do this, and some of them include integrating a chat feature for visitors who may have questions while browsing the site, forms that allow them to ask questions, email input for them to join a mailing list, receive a newsletter, video or a PDF, or even simply allowing them to ask for more information from you. This is where a great CTA can be crucial because it will provide the motivation for visitors to seek out more information than you've already provided them. The more visitors feel that they can interact with a site, the better because this also allows for a personalized feel. They aren't simply a name or a number, they're an individual.

Have an Enticing CTA

Today, people who use the Internet are used to being able to access information easily – and they may not want to give up their information without a good reason. Anyone can ask them to add their email address to a mailing list, or to provide information for a follow up… so you'll need to **make them understand that their time and information are valuable to you.** This can be done by offering something (typically for free) as discussed above, or even crafting a CTA that is targeted instead of vague. You need to prove to them that you're not just asking for their personal information without already having thought through the next steps – and how you can provide them with something that they want or need to succeed.

When thinking about the best ways to turn website visitors into leads, and then eventually into customers, there's a lot to consider. There's also a lot that can be overlooked, especially for those who are unfamiliar with the different parts of the marketing process and the best methods for appealing to these visitors.

To have a successful marketing strategy, all of the different aspects of it need to fit together and work well with one another because often these pieces flow from one to the next with very little pause in between them. For one piece to be successful and provide value, the previous one and the next one must do the same. Despite the fact that there is a clear, linear way that we imagine the inbounding process to go when it comes to obtaining new visitors and leads, the truth is that things don't always follow this order… and we need to prepare for it accordingly.

While a CTA is meant to motivate these visitors, it will only do so if it requests something very specific that they are looking for. A visitor isn't going to click on a button to be taken to a page that offers them something that they don't feel like they want or need. The idea behind a successful CTA is that by presenting it, you've given your visitors something to look forward to – or something to look **for.** The deeper a visitor gets within your page or site, the better, because this will expose them to different options, and more opportunities for conversion. In some cases, visitors will visit a site thinking that they are looking for one thing, but when presented with a different option, find that it suits their needs better.

Simply put, this CTA doesn't always need to be a flashy button or a standout graphic on the page. Contextual CTAs that are simply linked within another page text can be just as effective, as long as they're showing the visitor that by clicking, they will *get* something out of it.

CRAFT AND PRESENT THE RIGHT OFFER

Using quality CTAs also ties in with crafting and presenting the right type of offer. Any company can make promises to visitors and tell them that they'll be able to help them reach their goals… but it's not about simply dangling the bait and hoping for a bite. There are a few things that can be done in order to craft an offer that can't be refused, and it starts with remembering a few simple things.

- A good offer is something that people will actually want and be able to use in the future
- Compelling offers invite people in, but they're not hard sells and shouldn't feel like a sales pitch.
- Ensure that the offer provides a benefit. It doesn't have to be an immediate benefit, but it should be something that shows that it will *eventually* lead to one.

Crafting this offer doesn't have to be complex, but it needs to leave visitors feeling like it's not stock, not standard - not something that they could get from *anyone.*

USING FORMS TO CAPTURE USER INFORMATION

Once you've gotten the offers down and have created some compelling CTAs, it's time to consider how you'll best capture the data that site visitors and leads provide. Remember, getting them interested isn't often the difficult part - it's getting them interested *enough* to give you their contact information. Common ways that this information is caught and transmitted back to you is through the use of forms, which can be personalized to meet just about any marketing strategy with simple input options like email requests or even char windows.

When it comes to forms, it's important to remember that less is more at the beginning. Someone who is still deciding whether they believe that you can provide them with what they need won't want to give you an extensive amount of information and won't go *searching* for this form. This is where quality site design - especially on mobile devices - comes into play.

The first step in using forms properly for them to convert leads is to place them where they are *seen*. Even if the visitor is still deciding whether to fill it out, they know where to go if (when) they choose to do so. To be successful, your form should stand out, drawing the eye and making people *want* to utilize it.

PROVIDE VALUE TO CUSTOMERS WHO SHARE INFORMATION

Increasing the perceived value of providing the information and filling out the form is essential, too. Though this portion of a marketing strategy will differ depending on the type of form it is, people always want to believe that they are getting a great deal, even if it's for something simple and without actual monetary value.

Also consider only requiring relevant information for whatever the CTA or offer is. For example, for someone to receive access to a PDF file or a newsletter sign up, they won't want to spend longer than a minute or two providing their basic information. To start, a successful form will only ask users to give up the information that makes sense, but that still creates quality leads. Suggestions? Limit the fields on each form to only the ones that allow you to build a short client profile but won't make people pause before providing them. For example, don't always require a phone number, since so many people are wary of text or calls from unknown numbers.

Communicating with Perspective Clients

Site chats with live people may not always be possible 24/7, especially for smaller businesses, but giving visitors the option to reach out if they have questions or concerns is a great touch. Some chatbots can be programmed to answer the most common questions that site visitors have and can be used to put visitors into contact with actual representatives whenever possible. This is a great way to appeal to visitors, because not only does it show them that you're interested in what their individual questions are, but it also allows them to ask questions or schedule follow-up interactions on their own time. Chatting may not immediately lead to conversion, but it's a great start, and is another good way to capture email addresses along with names.

Offering visitors a chance to chat with someone instead of allowing them to feel as if they need to navigate the site and your offerings by themselves shows a good-faith investment on their part, as well as on yours. Even though they are simply *looking*, you're willing to guide them in the right direction.

This isn't just about giving your visitors value, either. Chat logs can be analyzed to see which questions visitors have, what they're looking for, and *where* they are reaching out from. This information can also lead to more pointed CTAs, a better location strategy, a new focus on keywords, and even more information about how long individual visitors remain on your page and how many times they visit. It's a simple feature to implement, but one that is very valuable overall.

Track Calls

Call tracking for local SEO is another important thing to consider because it allows us to see which avenues are producing the best and most consistent results. It may seem counterproductive to have different phone numbers associated with different marketing options, but this is recommended to see exactly what is working.

By having the ability to track calls, three things in particular can be done more effectively. We can see which areas are attracting the most visitors and producing the most leads. With this known, it will be possible to spend more time and effort on the angles of the campaign that are likely to see the most – and highest quality – results. This can result in increased ability for landing page optimization and keyword focus.

Moving forward, the other two huge benefits of call tracking are that it can be used to optimize the non-landing page leads that come in and that can help tell you how many visitors convert to leads and then eventually to customers. While it's important to focus on landing pages, as discussed above, sometimes it's another source that motivates the initial contact. The data that is gathered via this method can prove to be very valuable for businesses of all sizes and should be treated as such.

Dynamic Number Insertion (DNI)

One specific way to do this is to use dynamic number insertion software (DNI), which is a method that will insert a different number onto the page for each specific visitor, even though they all lead to the same end result. By using this method, it will be possible to track things like the keyword that was searched, the page that led to the call, the lead's phone number, where the caller is from and much, much more.

Conclusion

Converting traffic to customers is a process that takes time, since there are multiple steps and angles that must be considered, as well as considerations that must be made in order to effectively complete it. By following some of the steps and suggestions outlined here, you'll be well on your way to developing an effective strategy for attracting, enticing, and retaining these leads into lasting customers.

Chapter 33 includes a step-by-step guide for this process.

Section 5 – Resources

CHAPTER 30

SETTING UP
GOOGLE ANALYTICS

Sign into your Gmail account (if you do not have a Gmail account, visit Accounts.Google.com/SignUp and create a Google account). Remain signed in and create a google analytics account Marketing-Platform.Google.com/about/analytics/

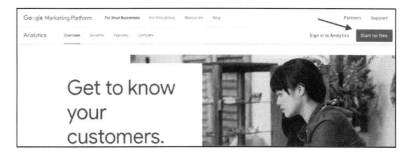

Click "Start for free" and fill out all the account information

- Account Name

- Company Name

- What do you want to measure?

- Unless you have an app choose "website"

- Website Name

- Using the company name again is fine

- Website URL

- Industry

REPORTING TIME

Click create

Once you have entered all the information and accepted the terms, a page will open that includes a global site tag code you need to install on your website so it can start tracking.

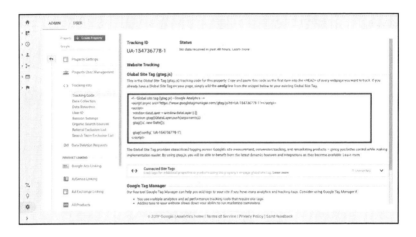

WORDPRESS SITES

1. Log into your WordPress site

2. Go to plugins

3. Activate "insert header footer scripts" plugin

4. Go to the plugin settings

5. Add the global site tag code into the header section

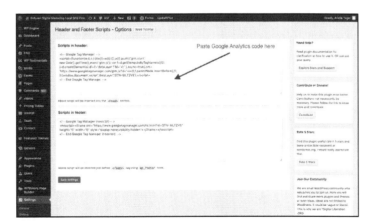

SHOPIFY SITES

1. Log into your Shopify site

2. Click on "online store"

3. Click "preferences"

4. There will be a google analytics box for you to paste the code

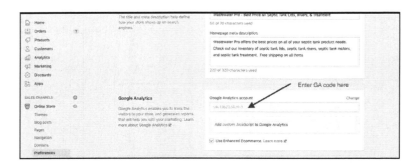

If you have any other website and do not know how to add a script into the header of the website, contact a developer. Once the code is installed, check back within 24 hours to make sure data has started flowing.

To share Google Analytics Access to an Agency

1. Login to Google Analytics

2. Click on bottom left hand corner gear icon "settings"

3. Click "account and user management"

4. Click the blue "+" circle button

5. Enter in the email of the person you want to provide access

6. Save

CHAPTER 31

Setting up the Google Search Console

Log into your Google account

1. Once you have a Google account, remain logged in and create a search console account https://search.google.com/search-console/about

2. Click start now

3. Under "domain" enter in the URL of your website

4. Your domain must be set to https BEFORE you setup your search console account

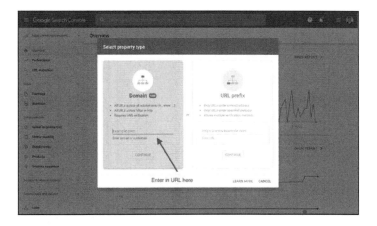

Once you enter your domain, it will tell you that you need to add a text file to your DNS instead of adding any code to your website. Because there's no code involved, this is the best method from a pure performance perspective. Google will provide instructions that look like this:

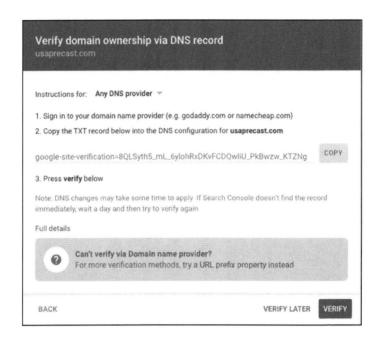

If you are unsure of how to add a .txt file to your DNS, research instructions based on your provider. In most cases, you simply login to your DNS, click manage, and click "add DNS record" and save.

If you cannot get into your DNS, you can follow the same steps of setting up a Search Console account except use the URL prefix property type instead of the domain property as the verification process is much easier.

Once you enter your URL into the prefix property, it will want you to auto verify your website. The easiest way to verify a website is by using Google Analytics. Once the global site tag from Google analytics is on your site, then it will auto verify. If you are still having trouble, visit Google's master guide for setting up Google Search Console here:

https://support.google.com/webmasters/answer/34592?hl=en

Once verified, check back within 48 hours to make sure data is flowing.

CHAPTER 32

SETTING UP A GOOGLE MY BUSINESS (GMB) LISTING

The main requirement to set up a Google My Business listing is a Gmail account. We recommend using a Gmail that is associated with your company name.

EXAMPLE:

Company Name: Enfusen Digital Marketing
Gmail: enfusen@gmail.com
Once you have your Gmail go to Google.com/Business and create an account.

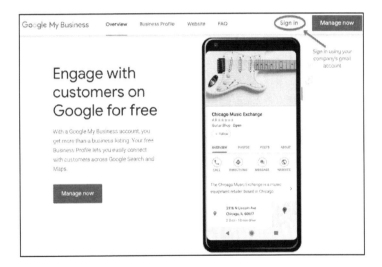

1. Type in the following business information

Business Name
Business Category
Business Location

2. Once you click submit, Google will notify you that in order to verify the listing, you will receive a postcard with a code to your business location within two weeks. When you receive the postcard, go back to your Google My Business listing and enter in the code to be officially verified.

3. Once you have an account, you can view your GMB easily by clicking on the square to the left of your Google icon and click on the "My Business" icon.

4. Once you have a verified GMB, we recommend adding as much business information as possible to increase the value. Some of the best things to add include

- Photos of your office building, team, and products/services

- Business short name

- Services that you offer

- Business hours

- Service areas

- Website URL

- Business description

CHAPTER 33

SETTING UP CALL TRACKING METRICS

1. Visit our Call Tracking Website to create an account. (RCBryan.com/Call-Tracking-Metrics)

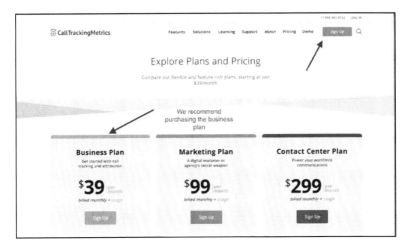

We recommend purchasing the Business Plan unless you are an extremely large organization. If you are confused about which package to purchase, please contact a member of our team.

2. Once signed up, navigate to the numbers section and click "buy numbers"

3. Under buy numbers, search for the area code that you want your phone number to have. If it's a local number, we recommend using the main city you service or where your business is located. If you are a national company, use the city listed on your GMB or a national number (1-800 or 1-888).

4. Once you find a number you like, click the "+" symbol to the right and purchase the number.

5. Once purchased, configure the number by adding the following:

-   Tracking source - Source of where the call is coming from
-   AdWords
-   Organic
-   Google My Business
-   The Target Number – This is the number you want the CTM code to search for on your website and swap with this number. This number is normally your main phone line for your company

6. Next, name the number and save

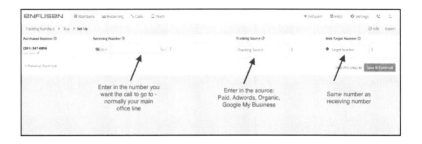

7. Continue this process until you have all the numbers you need.

8. Once you have purchased the numbers, add the CTM code to your website so it can start call swapping and tracking

9. Navigate in CTM to "numbers" and click on "tracking code"

10. Next, install the code onto the header of your website. We recommend using the plugin WordPress.org/plugins/header-and-footer-scripts/

11. Once the plugin is installed, navigate to "settings" and click on "header and footer scripts" In the header section, add the code from Call Tracking Metrics.

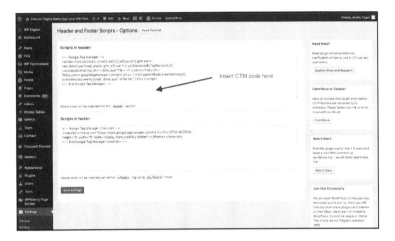

12. Make a test call and text search to ensure the number is swapping on your website (use incognito) and make a call to make sure it goes through. Then, check your CTM reporting dashboard to make sure the call was picked up by Call Tracking.

13. If you have issues, we recommend chatting with the CTM support.

CHAPTER 34

RUNNING A LOCAL CITATION AUDIT

To run a local citation audit, you need to finalize and confirm your Name, Address, and Phone Number (NAP).

Business Name
Address
Phone Number

Example

SEO Consultant Roger Bryan
526 South Main Street Suite 824 Akron Ohio 44311
888-994-4090

Then, run the citation audit in SEMRush

1. Login to SEMRush

2. On the left sidebar navigation click "listing management"

3. In the top right click "add location" green button"

Enter in your business information and click "check listings"

4. Click "distribute info" to submit your business information and start building citations

Once your info is submitted, it will take about 24 hours to fully distribute.

5. Add in more detailed information about your business. Go to your profile and click "edit info"

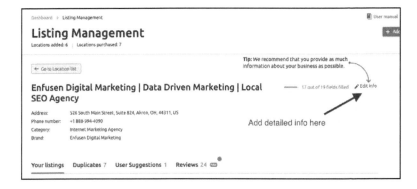

6.   Add information such as: Category (*Ex.*: Digital Marketing)

   Link your social and local channels (Facebook, Google My Business, Yelp Account)

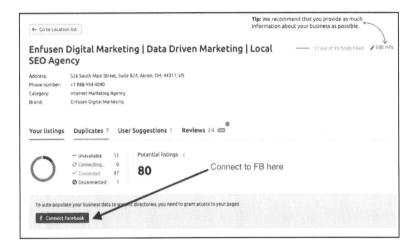

7.   Add your company logo and photos

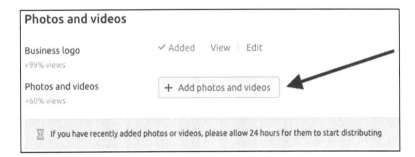

8. Add additional information, such as business description, business hours, and Website URL

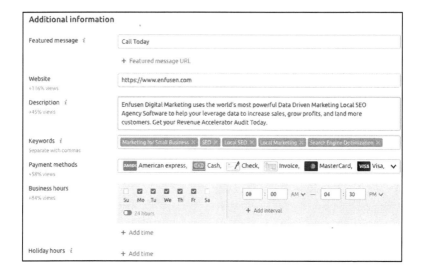

9. Save the information you entered and SEMRush will update accordingly over the next 24 hours.

We recommend you check on your citation campaign monthly and update if your business information changes.

CHAPTER 35

SETTING UP
AGENCY ANALYTICS

To get started using Agency Analytics, you will need to create an account. Once you sign up, follow the steps below to create your first campaign and dashboard.

1. Log into AgencyAnalytics.com

2. Under the dashboard view, click "Create Campaign"

3. Enter the following information

- Company Name
- Website Address (If possible, use the https version)
- Time Zone (Most users use the default time zone)
- Group (Optional)

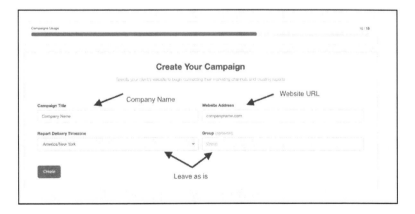

4. Select the integrations you want to connect to, beginning with at least the following:

- Google Analytics
- Google Search Console
- Google My Business
- Google Sheets

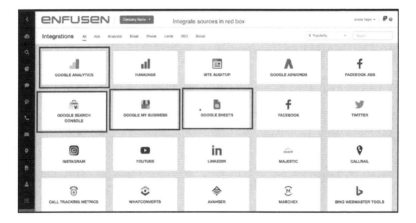

5. Click on "setup dashboard" to setup your first dashboard view

6. Click "use dashboard template"

7. Scroll all the way down the list and choose "Enfusen Offer Dashboard"

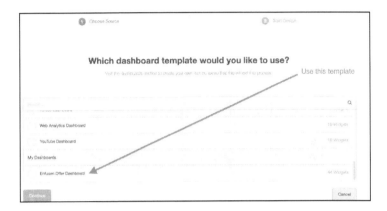

Once your dashboard is set up, you need to add 10-15 keywords to start understanding where your website rank is.

8. Using the left navigation panel click on "SEO" < then click on "rankings"

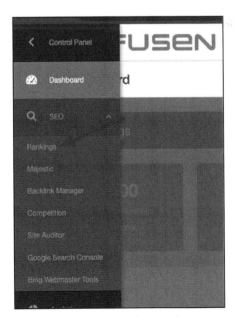

9. Under the Rankings dashboard, click "Add Keywords"

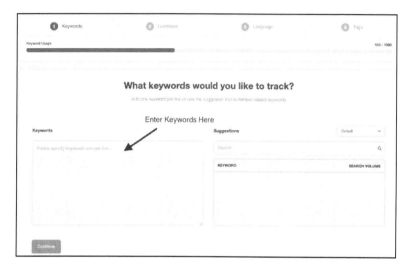

10. Enter the keywords you would like to track. **Example**: Aeration Septic

    Keywords Added: Septic inspection, septic service, septic inspector near me, septic tank inspection, septic tank inspectors near me, etc.

11. After entering your keywords, click "Continue" and choose your location. (If this is a national campaign (anyone can buy online), enter "United States of America.") If this is a local campaign where you have local service or a storefront, enter the main city where you work.

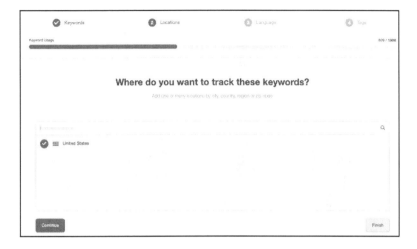

12. Use the default language

13. If you have multiple products or services, use tags. For example, some tags we use for Aeration Septic are:

- Septic inspection
- Septic service
- Septic tank installation
- Hydro-Action septic system
- County Keywords

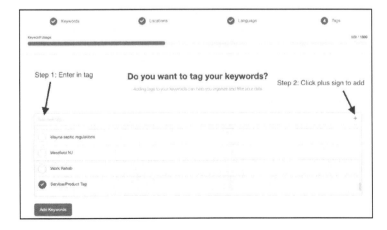

Once all keywords have been submitted, run the first site audit.

14. In the left-hand navigation panel, click on "site auditor"

15. Click "run audit"

16. Enter in the homepage of the website and click "run"

This process takes up to 24 hours, so make a note to check on it the following day.

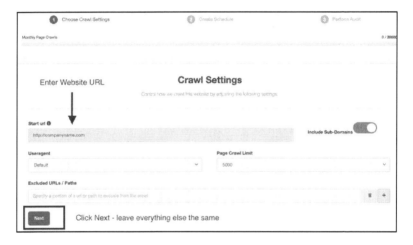

CREATING YOUR FIRST REPORT

1. Using the left navigation panel scroll down and click on "reports"

2. Click "Create Report"

3. Name the report "Company Name Report Template"

4. Choose "Report from template"

5. Choose "90 Day Campaign Performance Review"

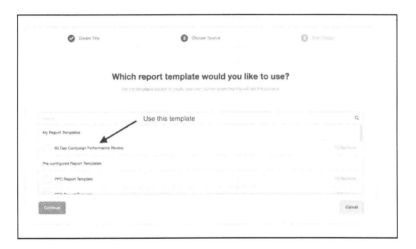

6. Choose the proper time frame and click save

By the end of the agency analytics setup process, you should have all data sources integrated, keywords added, a site audit running, a full dashboard, and a sample report.

CHAPTER 36

Glossary of SEO Terms

The Enfusen Digital Marketing Glossary

301 Redirect – A method of redirecting a visitor from one web page to another web page. This type of redirect is be used for permanent redirects (Example: you own websiteA.com and websiteB.com but you only want one website. You would 301 redirect all of the traffic from websiteB.com to websiteA.com so that all visitors end up on websiteA.com)

302 Redirect – A method of redirecting a visitor from one page to another web page; is used only for temporary situations. (For permanent redirects, use a 301 instead.)

404 Error – The error message that appears when a visitor tries to go to a web page that does not exist.

A

Ad Extensions – Additional pieces of information that can be added to Google AdWords ads, including reviews, address, pricing, callouts, app downloads, sitelinks, and click-to-call. Ad extensions help advertisers create richer, more informative ads that take up more on-page real estate, which generally lead to higher Click Through Rates.

Ad Manager Account – An advertising account on Facebook that allows you to run ads on the Facebook Ad Network.

Ad Network – A grouping of websites or digital properties (like apps) where ads can appear. For example, Google has 2 ad networks: the search network (text ads that appear in search results) and the display network (image ads that appear on millions of websites that have partnered with Google).

AdWords (Google AdWords) – A Google-owned program used by advertisers to place ads on Google search results pages, YouTube, and Google ad network sites. AdWords is the primary platform for PPC advertising.

Alt Text (or Alternative Text) – An attribute added to HTML code for images, used to provide vision impaired website visitors with information about the contents of a picture. Best practice dictates that all images on a website should have alt text, and that the text should be descriptive of the image.

Analytics (or Google Analytics) – A Google platform that allows webmasters to collect statistics and data about website visitors. Google Analytics (sometimes abbreviated as GA) allows webmasters to see where web traffic comes from and how visitors behave once on the site.

Anchor Text – The clickable words in a hyperlink. In SEO, anchor text is a ranking signal to Google, as it provides context about the destination site. For example, if many websites link to one particular website using the anchor text "free stock photos," Google uses that information to understand the destination site is likely a resource with free stock photos. Theoretically, that could help the stock photos website rank in Google for keywords related to stock photography.

AdSense (Google AdSense) – A Google platform that allows websites to earn money by publishing Google network ads on their website.

Algorithm – A process or set of rules that computers follow to perform a task. In digital marketing, algorithms usually refer to the sets of processes Google uses to order and rank websites in search results. The SEO industry gives various Google algorithms their own nicknames like Penguin (which analyzes the quality of links pointing to a website) and Panda (which assesses the quality of the content on a website). The main ranking algorithm is SEO is referred to as "The core algorithm."

Algorithm Update – A change made to a Google algorithm. Updates typically affect the rankings of websites. Google makes hundreds of adjustments to their algorithms throughout the year, as well as several major updates each year.

Alexa (Amazon Alexa) – Amazon's home assistant device that uses voice commands to do various things like play music, answer questions, give weather updates, and more. Voice search is becoming more interesting to the SEO industry as more people use devices like Alexa in place of computers for searches.

Automation – Using computer programs to perform repetitive tasks that would normally be completed by a human. Email programs can use automation to send email messages to people based on certain triggers (new customers, did or did not open the last email, etc.). Marketers also use automation to nurture leads by sending relevant content to previous visitors of a website in an attempt to get the visitor back to convert into a sale.

Average Position – A metric in Google AdWords that helps advertisers understand where, on average, their ads are showing in Google search results pages. There are usually 4 available ad slots at the top of a search result page (where 1 is the first ad, 2 is the second ad, etc.), so for the best results, advertisers typically want an average position between 1-4. Average position 5+ indicates that your ads are showing at the bottom of the search results page.

B

Backlink – Also known more plainly as a "link," this is when one website hyperlinks to another website using HTML href code. Backlinks are used by Google in their SEO ranking factors, with the basic idea being that if "website A" has incoming backlinks from other strong websites (websites B, C, and D), the links are votes of trust for website A, and website A gains some authority from B, C, and D through the links.

Banner Ad – A popular type of digital image ad that can be placed across various websites. The largest and most popular image ad network is run by Google and allows ads in the following common sizes:

250 x 250	Square
200 x 200	Small Square
468 x 60	Banner
728 x 90	Leaderboard
300 x 250	Inline Rectangle
336 x 280	Large Rectangle
120 x 600	Skyscraper
160 x 600	Wide Skyscraper
300 x 600	Half-Page Ad
970 x 90	Large Leaderboard

Bing – A web search engine that provides search services for web, video, image, and map search products. Bing is owned and operated by Microsoft and powers Yahoo! Search. Bing now controls approximately 20% of the search share.

Bing Ads – A platform that provides pay-per-click advertising on both the Bing and Yahoo! search engines. The service allows businesses to create ads and subsequently serve the ads to consumers who search for keywords that the businesses bid on. This platform also offers targeting options such as location, demographic, and device targeting.

Black Hat – Slang for an unethical digital marketer or SEO who uses spammy tactics to rank websites, like article spinning, mass directory link building, or negative SEO.

Blog – Short for "web log," a blog is a web page or a website that is regularly updated with new written content. Blogs are an important section of a website in digital marketing. They offer fresh new content on a regular basis, which can help attract new visitors, engage existing visitors, and give authority signals to Google.

Bot – An automated program that visits websites, sometimes referred to as a "crawler" or a "spider." A spam bot visits websites for nefarious reasons, often showing in Google Analytics as junk traffic. However, Google uses a bot to crawl websites so that they can be ranked and added to Google search.

Bounce Rate – The percentage of visitors to a website that leaves immediately without clicking or interacting with any portion of the page. For example, if 100 people visit a website, and 50 of them immediately leave, the website has a bounce rate of 50%. Websites aim to have a low bounce rate, and averages tend to be between 40-60%.

Breadcrumbs – Navigation links at the top of a web page that better help the user understand where they are on the website. These links often appear near the web page's title and look something like this: Home > Services > Specific Service

Business Manager – A Facebook platform that allows marketers to manage multiple pages and ad accounts in one central location.

C

Campaign – A series of advertising messages that share a theme and market a product or service. In the context of digital marketing, campaigns can be run through search and display network advertising platforms (i.e., Google, Bing), social media, email, or other online platforms.

Canonical (rel=canonical) – A piece of code added into the html head of a webpage to indicate to Google whether a piece of content is original or duplicated from somewhere else. Original content should be canonical to itself, and content taken from other places should point the canonical to the original source URL. Canonicals can also be used to avoid duplicate content issues within a website.

Click-Through-Rate (CTR) – A metric showing how often people click on an ad after they see it. You can calculate the CTR by dividing the number of clicks on the ad by the number of impressions (how many times it was seen). This ratio can be useful when determining whether an ad's messaging matches what the consumer is searching for and if it resonates with them.

Code – The languages used to build a website. The most commonly used languages in web design are HTML, CSS, JS, and PHP.

Contact Form – A section on a website with fillable fields for visitors to contact the website owner, most commonly used to collect names, phone numbers, and email addresses of potential customers.

Content – Any form of media online that users can read, watch, or interact with. Content commonly refers specifically to written material but can also include images and videos.

Conversion – The completion of a predefined goal. This is often used to track the number of site visitors who have been "converted" into paying customers, though sales are not always chosen as the metric. Other common goals are newsletter subscriptions and downloads of content from the website.

Conversion Rate – The rate at which visitors to a website complete the predefined goal. It is calculated by dividing the number of goal achievements by the total number of visitors. For example, if 100 people visit a website and 10 of them complete the conversion goal (like filling out a contact form), then the conversion rate is 10%.

Cost Per Acquisition (CPA) – A metric in paid advertising platforms that measures how much money is spent to acquire a new lead or customer. It can be calculated by dividing the total spend by the number of conversions for a given period of time. For example, if in a month, a PPC account spends $1000 and gets 10 conversions (leads), then the cost per acquisition is $100.

Cost Per Click (CPC) – The amount of money spent for a click on an ad in a Pay-Per-Click campaign. In the AdWords platform, each keyword will have an estimated click cost, but the prices change in real-time as advertisers bid against each other for each keyword. Average CPCs can range from less than $1 for longtail or low-competition keywords to upwards of $100 per click for competitive terms, primarily in legal, insurance, and water damage restoration industries.

Cost Per Thousand (CPM) – (*M is the roman numeral for 1,000*). The is the amount an advertiser pays for 1,000 impressions of their ad. For example, if a publisher charges $10 CPM, and your ad shows 2000 times, you will pay $20 for the campaign ($10 for 1000 impressions) x 2. Measuring ad success with CPM is most common in awareness campaigns, where impressions are more important than conversions or clicks.

Crawler – An automated software that scans websites. The name reflects how the software "crawls" through the code, which is why they are sometimes referred to as "spiders." Crawlers are used by Google to find new content and evaluate the quality of webpages for their index.

Conversion Rate Optimization (CRO) – A branch of digital marketing that aims to improve the conversion rate of web pages, making them more profitable. CRO combines psychology with marketing and web design to influence the behavior of the web page visitor. CRO uses a type of testing called "A/B split testing" to determine which version of a page (version A or version B) is more successful.

Cascading Style Sheets (CSS) – A CSS is a document of code that tells the website's HTML how it should appear on the screen. CSS is a time-saving document for web designers as they can style batched-sections of HTML code rather than styling individual lines of code one-at-a-time.

Call to Action (CTA) – An element on a web page used to push visitors towards a specific action or conversion. A CTA can be a clickable button with text, an image, or text, and typically uses an imperative verb phrase like: "Call Today" or "Buy Now."

D

Dashboard – A web page that contains and displays aggregate data about the performance of a website or digital marketing campaign. A dashboard pulls information from various data sources and displays the information in an easy-to-read format.

Digital Marketing – A catchall term for online work that includes specialized marketing practices like SEO, PPC, CRO, web design, blogging, content, and any other form of advertising on an internet-connected device with a screen. Traditionally, television was not considered digital marketing; however, the shift from cable television to internet streaming means that digital advertising can now be served to online TV viewers.

Directory – A website that categorically lists websites with similar themes. Some directories, like Chambers of Commerce (a list of businesses in a geographic area), can be helpful for SEO; however, widespread abuse of spam directories led Google to discount links from directories whose sole purpose was selling links.

Display Ads – Ads on a display network, which include many different formats such as images, flash, video, and audio. Also known as banner ads, these are the advertisements that are seen around the web on news sites, blogs, and social media.

Display Network – A network of websites and apps that display ads on their web pages. Google's display network spans over 2 million websites that reach over 90% of people on the internet. Businesses can target consumers on the display network based on keywords/topics, placement on specific webpages, and through remarketing.

Domain Name System (DNS) – A protocol that translates website URLs (which use alphabetic characters) into IP addresses (that use numeric characters). DNS exists because it is more useful for internet users to remember letters and words in website URLs, but the world wide web communicates in numbers with IP addresses. Without DNS, every website would just be a string of numbers rather than a traditional URL.

Dofollow – A phrase that denotes a hyperlink absent of a "nofollow" tag. By default, a hyperlink is a dofollow link until a "nofollow" piece of code is added to it. Dofollow links pass SEO equity to the destination URL, while "nofollow" links do not.

Duplicate Content – Refers to instances where portions of text are found in two different places on the web. When the same content is found on multiple websites, it can cause ranking issues for one or all of the websites, as Google does not want to show multiple websites in search results that have the exact same information. This type of duplicate content can occur because of plagiarism, automated content scrapers, or lazy web design. Duplicate content can also be a problem within one website — if multiple versions of a page exists, Google may not understand which version to show in search results, and the pages are competing against each other. This can occur when new versions of pages are added without deleting or forwarding the old version, or through poor URL structures.

E

Ecommerce (or E-Commerce) – A classification for businesses that conduct business online. The most common form of e-commerce business is an online retailer that sells products direct to the consumer.

Email Automation – A marketing system that uses software to automatically send emails based on defined triggers. Multiple automated emails in a sequence are used to create user funnels and segment users based on behavior. For example, an automation funnel could be set to send email 1 when a person provides their email address, then either email 2a or 2b would be sent based on whether the person clicked on the first email.

Email List – A collection of email addresses that can be used to send targeted email marketing campaigns. Lists are typically segmented by user classification so that a list of existing customers can receive one type of communication, while potential customers can receive more promotional communication.

Email Marketing – The use of email with the goal of acquiring sales, customers, or any other type of conversion.

F

Featured Snippet – A summarized piece of information that Google pulls from a website and places directly into search results to show quick answers to common and simple queries. Featured snippets appear in a block at the top of search results with a link to the source. Featured Snippets cannot be created by webmasters; Google programmatically pulls the most relevant information from an authoritative site. Most featured snippets are shown for question queries like "what is _____" or "who invented _____".

Facebook Advertising – Facebook allows advertisers to reach its users through their ad network. A range of ad types can be created to reach various goals set by companies. Facebook advertising is unique in that audiences are set up based on vast demographic information that Facebook has about their users, as compared to Google advertising that uses keywords.

Facebook Profile – A personal Facebook account. Profiles are automatically created when a user signs up for an account.

Facebook Business Page – A public webpage on Facebook created to represent a company. Using a business page gives users access to Facebook Ads Manager. It also allows businesses to engage with users (i.e., page likes, message responses, post content).

Facebook Ads Manager – Ads Manager is a tool for creating Facebook ads, managing when and where they'll run, and tracking how well campaigns are performing on Facebook, Instagram, or their Audience Network.

Form Fill – When a visitor has filled out a contact form on a website, commonly used as a noun to refer to a conversion. "This month, our marketing campaign generated 20 phone calls and eight form fills."

G

Google – Company behind the search engine giant Google.com. Founded in 1998, Google now controls approximately 80% of the search market. Google has also expanded to include many software services, both directly related to search, and targeted towards consumers outside of the search marketing industry like Google Chrome (a web browser), Google Fiber (internet service), Gmail (email client), and Google Drive (a file storing platform). Google is owned by parent company Alphabet.

Google Analytics – A free software platform created by Google, which is used to analyze nearly every aspect of users accessing a website. Website traffic, conversions, user metrics, historical data comparisons, and effectiveness of each channel of marketing can all be managed using this tool.

Google AdWords – Google's online advertising service. This system allows advertisers to reach customers through their search and display networks. AdWords offers several cost models which vary by bidding strategy and company goals. Advertisers can bid on keywords which allows their ads to show in Google search results and on Google's network of partner websites.

Google My Business – The platform on which businesses can input information to appear in search results, map packs, location searches, and more. Name, address, phone number, website link, hours of operation, and reviews can all be managed through this platform. GMB is crucial to local SEO campaigns, as this is directly related to location-based searches.

Google Partner Agency – An agency that is certified by Google after meeting certain requirements. To be a Google Partner, an agency must have an AdWords certified employee affiliated to the company profile, meet spend requirements, meet the performance requirement by delivering overall ad revenue and growth, and maintaining and growing the customer base.

Google Hummingbird – The industry nickname for one of the first major overhauls to the main Google search algorithm. In contrast to algorithm updates like Panda or Penguin, Hummingbird was intended to completely update the way Google interpreted user search queries. Previous to this update, Google results were mostly provided based on specific keyword matching within the user query. Now, a search for "Cheapest way to build birdhouses without using wood" will show results directly related to that query. Previously, users might see results that included wood as a building material. (See also: Google Algorithm, Google Panda, Google Penguin)

Google Home – A device for consumers that connects to their home network and can perform many basic tasks through voice commands. Typical uses for Google Home include asking basic questions, making Google searches, scheduling appointments, playing music, or setting alarms.

Google Maps – The location and navigation service provided by Google. Using maps.Google.com, users can search for stores, restaurants, businesses, and landmarks anywhere in the world. Typically, users will find routes to nearby establishments including local businesses using Maps.

Google Panda – A Google algorithm update focused on analyzing the quality of a website's on-page content. Initially released February 2011, and updated periodically after this release, similar to Google Penguin. This update would determine if content on site pages was related to queries it was being displayed for and alter the site's rankings accordingly. Sites with low-quality content saw significant ranking drops due to this algorithm update. The algorithm has now been assimilated to Google's core search algorithm and can assess content quality in real time. (See also: Google Algorithm, Google Penguin)

Google Penguin – A Google algorithm update focused on analyzing the quality of links pointing to a site, or more accurately, the overall quality of a site's backlink profile. First announced in April 2012 and updated periodically after this release, similar to Google Panda. This algorithm targeted so-called "black-hat SEO" tactics which manipulated search rankings by creating links to sites in an unnatural manner. Google analyzes all of the pages that link to a specific site and determine whether the links are a benefit to users, or if they simply serve to manipulate search rankings and adjust the site's standing accordingly. Google estimates that Penguin affects 3.1% of all searches in English, a relatively large number for one algorithm. (See also: Backlink, Black Hat, Google Algorithm, and Google Panda).

Google Pigeon – A Google algorithm update focused on providing locally relevant results to searchers. For example, searching for "SOHO coffee shop" will return results primarily centered around that neighborhood. In addition, Google can determine your location when you enter a search and show you local businesses nearby your area even without localized keywords. This algorithm greatly influenced the potential for local businesses to appear in search results. (See also: Google Algorithm)

Google Algorithm – A mathematical programmatic system that determines where websites will appear on Google search result pages for any given number of queries. Sometimes called the "Core" algorithm, though this is a less specific term. Google's algorithm is constantly updated (approximately 500-600 times per year, or two times per day), which can have varying levels of impact on the rankings of websites across the world. Google's actual algorithm is deliberately kept secret to prevent webmasters from manipulating the system for rankings, though Google does publicly state their suggested "best practices" for appearing higher in search results.

Google Reviews – Reviews left using the Google My Business platform. Reviews are on a 1- to 5-star scale and include a brief message written by the reviewer. Reviews can show up in the knowledge graph in Google searches and have been shown to positively correlate with SEO rankings. (See also: Google My Business)

Google Search Console (formerly Webmaster Tools) – A free tool Google offers to webmasters. Within the tool are several areas that include data on how a site is performing in search. Search Console differs from Analytics in that it does not measure traffic; it measures a site's visibility on search pages, and indexability by Google crawler bots. Search Console measures metrics such as Click-Through Rate, Number of Indexed Pages, Number of Dead Links (AKA 404 pages), and more. (See also: Google Analytics, Click-through rate, Index, Crawler/Spider)

Google Click IDentifier GCLID – A small string of numbers and letters that serves as a unique ID badge for visitors to a website. Typically, this is used to keep track of individual users as they click on a PPC ad, so that their interaction with the website (whether they converted, on which page, and using which method) can be tracked and attributed properly using Google Analytics. (See also: Google Analytics, PPC)

Gravity Forms – A WordPress plugin that adds a customizable contact form to a website. This plugin keeps track of all completed form submissions and allows for all of the fields on a form to be customized.

H

Help A Reporter Out (HARO) – Three times a day Monday through Friday, HARO emails are sent out, listing different stories for which reporters need sources. Used as a marketing strategy to gain PR and link opportunities.

Hashtag – A phrase beginning with the symbol "#" used in social media as a way for tagging content for users to find. Adding hashtags to a post allows users to find that post when searching for that topic. This can be used for finding users looking for broad topics on social media, as well as niche, detailed topics.

Header – Can refer to either the top portion of a webpage that typically contains the logo and menu, or the section of HTML in a website's code that contains important information about the site.

Header Code – On a website, certain code is placed in the universal header section so that it can be accessible across all pages of the website. Typically, in the header code, you'll find things like Schema Markup, Analytics Code, AdWords Code, and other tools used for tracking data across a website. These are placed in the header code so that they can be rendered and start tracking information as the site loads.

Header Tags (H1, H2, H3, etc.) – Header tags are used in HTML for categorizing text headings on a web page. They are, in essence, the titles and major topics of a web page and help indicate to readers and search engines what the page is about. Header tags use a cascading format where a page should have only one H1 (main title) but beneath can be multiple H2s (subtitles) and every H2 can have H3s beneath (sub-subtitles) and so on.

- H1 is used only once on a webpage to display the most important title.
- H2 is used to display the major subtopics of a certain webpage
- H3 is used to display the major subtopics underneath H2 tags.

Heatmap – A graphical representation of how users interact with your site. Heat Mapping software is used to track where users click on a page, how they scroll, and what they hover over. Heatmaps are used to collect user behavior data to assist in designing and optimizing a website.

Hypertext Markup Language (HTML) – A set of codes that are used to tell a web browser how to display a webpage. Each individual code is called an element, or a tag. HTML has a starting and ending element for most markups.

Hypertext Transfer Protocol (HTTP) – The protocol used by the world wide web to define how data is formatted and transmitted, and what actions web browsers and web servers should take to respond to a command. When you enter a website into your web browser and press enter, this sends an HTTP command to a web server, which tells the server to fetch and send the data for that website to your browser.

Hypertext Transfer Protocol Secure (HTTPS) – A secured version of HTTP, which is used to define how data is formatted and transmitted across the web. HTTPS has an advantage over HTTP in that the data sent when fetching a web page is encrypted, adding a layer of security so that third parties can't gather data about the webpage when the data is sent from the server to the browser.

Hreflang Tag – A code in the HTML of a website that tells search engines like Google which spoken language a web page is using. These are especially useful for websites that have versions of pages in multiple languages, as they help Google understand which pages are related and which should be shown to specific audiences.

Hummingbird – See "Google Hummingbird."

Hyperlink – A hyperlink is an HTML code that creates a link from one webpage to another web page, characterized often by a highlighted word or image that takes you to the destined location when you click on that highlighted item.

I

Iframe – An HTML document that is inside of another HTML document on a website. Iframes are commonly used to embed content from one source onto another web page.

Impression – A term used in Pay per click advertising that represents how many times an ad was shown.

Impression Share – Used in Pay per click advertising, this metric refers to the percentage of times viewers have seen an advertiser's ad, in relation to the total possible amounts that ad could have been seen. If an ad campaign's impression share is 70%, then the ads showed 7 out of 10 possible times.

Inbound Marketing – Inbound marketing refers to the activities and strategies used for attracting potential users or customers to a website. "Inbound" is a more recent euphemism for what has traditionally been called "SEO." Inbound marketing is crucial to having a good web presence, as it's used to attract prospective customers by educating and building trust about your services, product and/or brand. (See also: organic)

Index – When used as a noun, index refers to all of the web pages that Google has crawled and stored to be shown to Google searchers (e.g., "The Google index has billions of websites"). When used as a verb, it refers to the act of Google copying a web page into their system (e.g., "Google indexed my website today so it will start appearing in their search results").

Internet Protocol (IP) Address – A unique number that identifies a device using the internet to communicate over a network. Each device has a unique IP address, and can be used to locate and differentiate that device from all other devices when using the internet. You can find your public IP address by going to Google and searching "What is my IP address."

J

Java – A programming language used to create applications that can run on a digital device. Java can be used on its own, while JavaScript can only be used in web browsers.

JavaScript (JS) – A scripting language used on web browsers to provide interactive elements to web pages that are difficult or impossible to achieve with just HTML or CSS.

K

Keyword – A word or phrase indicative of the major theme in a piece of content. When you search for something in a search engine, you type in a keyword and the search engine gives you results based on that keyword. One major goal of SEO is to have your website appear in search results for as many keywords as possible.

Keyword Phrase – A group of two or more words that are used to find information in a search engine. Sometimes, when searching for something, one single keyword does not provide the information you seek, but a keyword phrase allows you to string multiple words together to find better information.

Keyword Density – The percentage of how often a keyword appears on a webpage in relation to the total words on that webpage.

Keyword Stuffing – When a web page uses a keyword too often or superfluously, with the intent of manipulating search engines. This type of behavior is frowned upon and can lead to either algorithmic devaluation in search, or a manual penalty from Google.

L

Landing Page – The destination webpage a user lands on after clicking on a link (either in an ad or anywhere else). Some landing pages are designed with the purpose of lead generation, and others with the purpose of directing the flow of traffic throughout a site.

Latent Semantic Indexing (LSI) – A search engine indexing method that creates a relationship between words and phrases to form a better understanding of a text's subject matter. Latent semantic indexing helps search engines serve up results to queries with higher precision.

Lead – A potential customer in the sales funnel who has communicated with a business with intent to purchase through a call, email, or online form fill.

Link – Also known as a hyperlink, a link is a string of hypertext transfer protocol structured text used to connect web pages on the internet. There are two main forms of links: internal links that point to pages on the same site, and external links that point to web pages on a different website.

Link Profile – The cumulative grouping of all links pointing to a particular website. A link profile can be used to determine a website's power, trust, subject matter, and content. Link profiles are important at determining where a website ranks in google search results. If a website has a high number of links from websites that are not trusted, adult in nature, spammy, or against guidelines, the link profile will have a negative effect on rankings. If a website has a high number of links from websites that are strong providers of content or reputable sources of information, it will have a positive effect on rankings.

LinkedIn – A social networking website oriented around connecting professionals to jobs, businesses and other professionals in their industry. LinkedIn is also a strong platform for marketing, job posting, and sharing professional content.

LinkedIn Advertising – LinkedIn's advertising platform. Through different ad formats, advertisers can bid on ad space and target unique audiences based on job title, years of experience, industry, and many other demographics.

Link Network – A black hat link building strategy that uses a network of websites all interconnected with links to boost backlink profiles and rank certain sites higher in google search results. Some link networks can also be known as private blog networks (PBNs). Link networks and PBNs are against Google guidelines and are devalued or penalized when detected.

Lookalike Audience – A targeting option offered by Facebook's ad service. This audience is created from a source audience (i.e., fans of your Facebook page, email list) and from this list, Facebook will identify common characteristics between audience members. Facebook will then target users that exhibit similar interests or qualities.

Long Tail Keyword – A keyword phrase that is longer in length and hyper-specifically matches a user search query. A long tail keyword gets less searches per month but has a higher search intent and typically less competition by companies looking to serve up content to that search query. For example, a regular keyword might be "Austin web designer" but a long tail keyword would be "affordable Austin web designer that makes WordPress sites."

M

Map Pack – The section of Google search results pages featuring three businesses listed in a local map section. The map pack shows up for queries with local intent, a general business type, or a "near me" search.

Medium (source/medium) – The general category of traffic to a website tracked in Google analytics. Some examples of common medium are:

- Organic
- CPC
- Email
- Referral

Meta Tags – HTML snippets added to a webpage's code that add contextual information for web crawlers and search engines. Search engines use meta data to help decide what information from a webpage to display in their results. Example meta tags include the date the page was published, the page title, author, and image descriptions.

Meta Description – One of the meta tags that gives a description of the page in 160 characters. The meta description is an important aspect of a webpage because it is what appears in Google searches and other search engine results.

Meta Keywords – A specific meta tag that displays the specific keywords addresses in a page. After meta keyword markup was abused on some websites, listed keywords no longer apply to how a page is categorized by google and other search engines.

N

Name, Address, Phone Number (NAP) – Acronym for local citations. Consistency in name, address, and phone number citations is an important piece of a local SEO Campaign. To build local SEO authority, a business's name, address, and phone number should be listed across local citation websites like Yelp, Google Business, Angie's List, Yellow Pages, Better Business Bureau, Foursquare, and more.

Nofollow – An HTML link attribute that communicates to web crawlers and search engines that the link to the destination web page should NOT transfer SEO equity (i.e., it shouldn't give SEO benefit to the recipient). According to Google's guidelines, any link that is unnatural (like you paid for a press release, or you gave a journalist a perk for writing about your product) should have a nofollow tag.

O

Organic – A source of traffic to a website that comes through clicking on a non-paid search engine result. Organic traffic is a main measurement of an SEO campaign and grows as a site ranks better for keywords or ranks for more keywords in search engines.

P

Panda – A search engine algorithm developed by Google to rate the quality and relevance of content on a webpage. Google Panda was released in February 2011 and devalued sites in search results that had thin, non-original, or poorly written content.

Private Blog Network (PBN) – Also known as a link network, a private blog network is a collection of private websites all linking to each other. These networks are intended to manipulate search engines by adding large amounts of new links to a website's link profile.

Penguin – A search engine algorithm developed by Google to determine the quality of links pointing to a particular site. It was launched to deter spammers from blackhat SEO practices, such as private blog and link networks. Google Penguin was released in April 2012 and updated regularly until 2016 when it was then rolled into the Core Algorithm.

Pigeon – A Google search engine algorithm intended to serve up locally targeted information for certain searches. Google Pigeon was released on July 24, 2014 and helps users find local businesses from broad keyword searches.

Pay-Per-Click (PPC) – An online advertising model in which advertisers are charged for their ad once it is clicked. The PPC model is commonly associated with search engine and social media advertising like Google AdWords and Facebook Ads.

Position – The placement in Google search results that a site is in for a specific query.

- **Featured Snippet**: When content within a web page is pulled into Google search results to instantly give the information a user is looking for.

- **First Page**: When a site ranks on the first page of Google search results.

- **Map Pack**: The first through third result on a Google SERP result page that serves up local businesses for a query.

Penalty – An infraction issued by Google to a webmaster for breaking Google's guidelines. The penalty is issued by Google through Search Console and can result removal of the site from search engine results. The issues that caused the penalty will need to be fixed before the penalty is lifted, and once the penalty is lifted it may still take some time to return to previous rank in Google search results. Penalty may also refer to an "algorithmic penalty" which is actually a misnomer; a website may be doing poorly in search results because of an issue that Google's algorithm has found in the site. This however is not really a "penalty" but a ranking problem. For there to be a true penalty, there would have to be a manual action from Google, as denoted by the message sent to the webmaster in Search Console.

PDF – A digital document format that provides a digital image of text or graphics. PDFs are the preferred document type when uploading documents to the internet because of its ease of use and its ability to be imported or converted easily. PDFs can be read and indexed by Google just as a normal web page can.

Q

Quality Score – Google AdWords' rating of the relevance and quality of keywords used in PPC campaigns. These scores are largely determined by relevance of ad copy, expected click-through rate, and the landing page quality and relevance. Quality score is a component in determining ad auctions, so having a high score can lead to higher ad rankings at lower costs.

Query – The term given for what a user types and searches using search engines like Google, Bing, and Yahoo. Examples of queries include "Austin electrician," "How do I know if I have a raccoon in my attic," "Distance to nearest coffee shop," and many more.

R

Rankings – A general term for where a website appears in search engine results. A site's "ranking" may increase or decrease over time for different search terms or queries. Ranking is specific to each keyword, so a website may have keywords that rank on the first page and others that don't.

Reciprocal Link – Two websites linking to each other, typically for the express purpose of increasing the search engine ranking for both. These types of links are sometimes deemed manipulative by search engines, which can incur a penalty or devaluation against both sites.

Redirect – A way by which a web browser takes a user from one page to another without the user clicking or making any input. There are various types of redirects (the most common of which is the 301 redirect), which serve different purposes. Typically, this helps improve user experience across a website.

Referral – A medium denoted in Google Analytics that represents a website visit that came from another website (as opposed to coming from a Google search, for example). When users click on a link to another, external webpage, they are said to have been "referred" there.

Rel Canonical – In HTML, "rel" is an attribute associated with links. "Canonical" can be applied to the "rel" attribute, which will link to the original or authoritative page from which content is being used or referenced. The "canonical" page is the original content, and any page referencing it is a duplicate or otherwise similar page. Used to prevent duplicate content issues and maintain search engine rankings.

Remarketing – Also known as retargeting, a type of paid ad that allows advertisers to show ads to customers who have already visited their site. Once a user visits a site, a small piece of data called a "cookie" will be stored in the user's browser. When the user then visits other sites, this cookie can allow remarketing ads to be shown. Remarketing allows advertisers to "follow" users around in attempts to get the user back to the original site.

Responsive Web Design – A philosophy of creating a website that allows all of the content to show correctly regardless of screen size or device. Your website will "respond" to the size of the screen each user has, shrinking and reorganizing on smaller screens, and expanding to fill appropriately on large ones.

Return on Ad Spend (ROAS) – A PPC marketing metric that demonstrates the profit made as compared to the amount of money spent on the ads. Similar to ROI.

Robots.txt – A text file stored on a website's server that includes basic rules for indexing robots which "crawl" the site. This file allows you to specifically allow (or disallow) certain files and folders from being viewed by crawler bots, which can keep your indexed pages limited to only the pages you wish.

Return on Investment (ROI) – For a business to receive a positive ROI, they must earn more money using marketing channels than they are spending on the marketing itself.

Really Simple Syndication (RSS) – A way for users to keep track of updates to multiple websites (news sites, blogs, and more) in one place, instead of having to manually check every single site individually. An RSS Feed is a place where all updates are tracked together, in an easily viewable format.

S

Schema Markup – Code that is added to the HTML of a website to give search engines more relevant information about a business, person, place, product, or thing (also known as rich snippets or structured data).

Search Network – A group of websites in which ads can appear. Google's Search Network, for example, is a group of Google and non-Google websites that partner with Google to show text ads.

Search Engine – A program that searches an index of information and returns results to the user based on corresponding keywords. The most well-known search engines are Google, YouTube, Bing, and Yahoo.

Search Operator – A text modifier that can be used in Google searches to return more specific results. Search operators essentially act as shortcuts to an advanced search.

Search Engine Marketing (SEM) – A nebulous term that can apply to either 1.) Any digital marketing that involves the use of a search engine, or 2.) Only paid digital marketing that involves a search engine, i.e., PPC (pay-per-click). There is not an industry standard as to which definition is correct, however, the latter is most commonly used.

Search Engine Optimization (SEO) – The process of improving a website's performance and positioning in organic search engine results through a variety of methodologies including content production or improvement, technical and code improvement, and link acquisition.

Search Engine Results Page (SERP) – The page featuring a list of search results that is returned to the searcher after they submit a keyword search.

Sessions – A metric in Google Analytics that measures one user interacting with a website during a given period of time, which Google defaults to 30 minutes. A session is not dependent on how many pages are viewed, so if a person goes to a website and looks around at different pages for 20 minutes, it would count as one session.

Siri – Apple's voice search technology that allows for hands-free searching on iPhones and other Apple products.

Sitelink – An ad extension in Google AdWords that appears below the main ad copy which links to a specific page on the website (i.e., Contact Us, About Us, etc.). Ads can have 2-6 sitelinks.

Sitemap – An XML file or page on a website that lists all of the pages and posts for search engines to see. This document helps search they should be aware of on a particular website.

Slug – Slang for the portion of a URL that comes after the ".com." For example, the homepage might be http://www.domain.com, but for the Contact Us page, a slug would be added to the end of the URL to direct the browser to a page within the website, such as http://www.domain.com/contact-us.

Source – A term in Google Analytics that helps webmasters classify where traffic is coming from (i.e., the "source" of the web traffic). Source can be a search engine (for example, Google) or a domain (website-example.com)

Spam – A broad term that includes many different nefarious activities in digital marketing that are done either to help a website rank better or to harm a competitor website. Spam is often seen in the form of hundreds or thousands of low-quality backlinks that were built by a black hat SEO to manipulate rankings.

Spider – An automated program that visits websites, sometimes also referred to as a "crawler" or a "bot." A spam spider visits websites for nefarious reasons, often showing in Google Analytics as junk traffic. However, Google uses a bot to crawl websites so that they can be ranked and added to Google search.

Style Sheet – Shortened term for Cascading Style Sheet (CSS). CSS a document of code that tells the website's HTML how it should appear on screen. CSS is a time-saving document for web designers as they can style batched-sections of HTML code, rather than styling individual lines of code one-at-a-time.

T

Tag – In WordPress, a tag is an identifying marker used to classify different posts based on keywords and topics. These are similar to WordPress categories, but more granular and specific, whereas categories are broad and thematic.

Title Tag – An HTML element used to describe the specific topic of a web page. Title tags are displayed in the tabbed top bar of a web browser. In SEO, it is best practice to have descriptive title tags featuring your main keywords, rather than something basic like "Home."

Tracking Code – A script, often placed in the header, footer, or thank you page of a website that passes information along to software tools for data gathering purposes. Tools like Google Analytics and Google AdWords utilize tracking codes to track information about users who view a site.

Twitter – A social media platform where users interact or "tweet" by posting a message or replying to a message using 280 characters or less. Each keystroke on a keyboard is considered a character. Twitter is used to share information and links and utilizes hashtags to categorize information. Tweets are typically public and can be seen by anyone. If you are followed by another user, that user will see your tweets in their feed. Similarly, you will see the tweets of anyone you follow in your feed.

Twitter Advertising – Allows marketers to promote a tweet on users' feeds without requiring that user to follow your brand for it to appear on their feed. These advertisements can be used to grow brand awareness, gain more followers, extend social media reach, or reach out to prospective customers about a product or service.

U

Uniform Resource Locator (URL) – The web page address. The URL refers to what specific web page a web browser is viewing.

Unique Visitors -A metric used in web analytics to show how many different, unique people view a website over a period of time. Unique visitors are tracked by their IP addresses. If a visitor visits the same website multiple times, they will only be counted once in the unique visitor's metric.

User Interface (UI) – UI is the area with which a user interacts with something through a digital device. Good UI should be fluid and easy for most people to understand.

User Experience (UX) –UX refers to how a user interacts with a website or app (where they click, which pages they visit). UX can be shaped by testing differences in page layouts, CTAs, colors, content, etc. to improve conversion rates. Having a good UX is crucial to having a good business, as it drives repeating users and engagement.

V

Visits – An old term in Google Analytics that was recently changed to "sessions."

Visitors – A metric in Google Analytics that quantifies a user of a website over a particular period of time. Visitors are often broken down between "new visitors" who are browsing for the first time in the allotted time period or "returning visitors" who have already browsed at least once in the given time frame.

W

Web 2.0 – The second major phase of development of the World Wide Web, marked by a shift from static web pages to dynamic content, as well as social media and user-generated content.

Website – A document or group of documents that are accessible on the World Wide Web.

Webinar – An online seminar used to train, inform, or sell to an audience of viewers who signed up to view the presentation.

White Hat – Term for ethical digital marketers who don't participate in work that could be viewed as unethical or as spam.

Wireframe – A cursory layout drawing of a webpage that acts as the first step in the design process.

X

XML (eXtensible Markup Language) – Like HTML (Hypertext Markup Language), it is primarily used to categorize various data for computers and humans to use more effectively. In basic terms, XML allows for customizable tags for marking up information that is otherwise difficult for computers to understand.

XML Sitemap – A document in XML format that categorizes all relevant pages, posts, files, etc. of a website. This document is not intended for human use, though humans can view it. Instead, an XML sitemap is designed to help search engine crawler bots easily find all of the pages for a given website – very similar to a roadmap or atlas that one would use when driving a car long distances.

Y

Yelp – A social review platform and search engine that allows users to leave reviews for businesses. Yelp also offers an advertising program that gives advertisers the ability to show their marketing assets to qualified Yelp users based on keyword searches.

YouTube – A video-sharing website, bought by Google in 2006. YouTube is part of Google's ad network and is currently the 2nd most used search engine in the world.

YouTube Advertising – YouTube offers advertising in six different formats: display ads, overlay ads, skippable video, non-skippable video ads, bumper ads, and sponsored cards. These ads can all be created and run through the Google AdWords platform.

Yahoo! Search – The third largest search engine in the US, owned by Yahoo. Since 2009, the engine has been powered by Bing.

Yahoo! Advertising – Yahoo and Bing ads are both run through the Bing Ads platform. These search engines share advertising networks.

Printed in Poland
by Amazon Fulfillment
Poland Sp. z o.o., Wrocław

25586284R00143